Ivan Moscovich's
Mastermind Collection

Tough Topology Problems & Other Puzzles

Sterling Publishing Co., Inc.
New York

To Anitta, Hila, and Emilia, with love

Ivan Moscovich Mastermind Collection:
Tough Topology Problems & Other Puzzles was edited, designed, and typeset by
Imagine Puzzles Ltd., London (info@imaginepuzzles.com)

MANAGING EDITOR
David Popey
ART EDITOR
Keith Miller
CONSULTANT EDITOR
David Bodycombe
PROJECT EDITOR
Marilyn Inglis
EDITORIAL ASSISTANT
Rosemary Browne
PUBLISHING DIRECTOR
Hal Robinson

Clipart: Nova Development Corporation

Library of Congress Cataloging-in-Publication Data Available

2 4 6 8 10 9 7 5 3 1

Published by Sterling Publishing Co., Inc.
387 Park Avenue South, New York, NY 10016
© 2006 by Ivan Moscovich
Distributed in Canada by Sterling Publishing
c/o Canadian Manda Group, 165 Dufferin Street
Toronto, Ontario, Canada M6K 3H6
Distributed in the United Kingdom by GMC Distribution Services
Castle Place, 166 High Street, Lewes, East Sussex, England BN7 1XU
Distributed in Australia by Capricorn Link (Australia) Pty. Ltd.
P.O. Box 704, Windsor, NSW 2756, Australia

Sterling ISBN-13: 978-1-4027-2732-0
ISBN-10: 1-4027-2732-1

For information about custom editions, special sales, premium and corporate purchases, please
contact Sterling Special Sales Department at 800-805-5489 or specialsales@sterlingpub.com

Contents

Introduction

Ever since my high school days I have loved puzzles and mathematical recreational problems. This love developed into a hobby when, by chance, some time in 1957, I encountered the first issue of *Scientific American* with Martin Gardner's mathematical games column. And for the past 50 years or so I have been designing and inventing teaching aids, puzzles, games, toys, and hands-on science museum exhibits.

Recreational mathematics is mathematics with the emphasis on fun, but, of course, this definition is far too general. The popular fun and pedagogic aspects of recreational mathematics overlap considerably, and there is no clear boundary between recreational and "serious" mathematics. You don't have to be a mathematician to enjoy mathematics. It is just another language, the language of creative thinking and problem-solving, which will enrich your life, like it did and still does mine.

Many people seem convinced that it is possible to get along quite nicely without any mathematical knowledge. This is not so: Mathematics is the basis of all knowledge and the bearer of all high culture. It is never too late to start enjoying and learning the basics of math, which will furnish our all-too sluggish brains with solid mental exercise and provide us with a variety of pleasures to which we may be entirely unaccustomed.

In collecting and creating puzzles, I favor those that are more than just fun, preferring instead puzzles that offer opportunities for intellectual satisfaction and learning experiences, as well as provoking curiosity and creative thinking. To stress these criteria, I call my puzzles Thinkthings.

The *Mastermind Collection* series systematically covers a wide range of mathematical ideas, through a great variety of puzzles, games, problems, and much more, from the best classical puzzles taken from the history of mathematics to many entirely original ideas. This book, *Tough Topology Puzzles and Other Problems,* deals with shape and area relationships.

A great effort has been made to make all the puzzles in this book understandable to everybody, though finding some of the solutions may be hard work. For this reason, the ideas are presented in a highly esthetic visual form, making it easier to perceive the underlying mathematics.

I hope that these books will convey my enthusiasm for and fascination with mathematics and share these with the reader. They combine fun and entertainment with intellectual challenges, through which a great number of ideas, basic concepts common to art, science, and everyday life, can be enjoyed and understood.

Some of the games included are designed so that they can easily be made and played. The structure of many is such that they will excite the mind, suggest new ideas and insights, and pave the way for new modes of thought and creative expression.

Despite the diversity of topics, there is an underlying continuity in the topics included. Each individual Thinkthing can stand alone (even if it is, in fact, related to many others), so you can dip in at will without the frustration of cross-referencing.

I hope you will enjoy the *Mastermind Collection* series and Thinkthings as much as I have enjoyed creating them for you.

—Ivan Moscovich

Common sense tells us that Achilles should win this race, but if we believe the logic of Zeno's paradox, then the opposite is true. Can you find the flaw in Zeno's logic?

▼ ZENO'S PARADOX

The famous mathematician Zeno, born in Italy around 490 B.C.*, created over 40 paradoxes to defend the teachings of the philosopher Parmenides, his teacher, who believed in* monism: *that reality was unchanging, and that change (motion) was impossible. His puzzling paradoxes seemed impossible to resolve at the time.*

  The most famous of Zeno's paradoxes is the race between Achilles and the tortoise. In the race, Achilles gives the tortoise a head start; Zeno's argument goes like this:

  When Achilles reaches the point (A) where the tortoise started, the tortoise has crawled to a new point (B). Now Achilles must run to point B to catch up with the tortoise. But in the meantime the tortoise has moved to point C, and so on.

Start
Achilles

> **O**nly two things are infinite, the universe and human stupidity, and I'm not sure about the former.
> *Albert Einstein*

Zeno's conclusion was that it would take Achilles an infinite amount of time to catch the tortoise. Achilles gets closer and closer, but he never catches up with the tortoise; his journey is divided into an infinite number of pieces. Before a moving object can travel a certain distance, it must travel half that distance. Before it can travel half the distance it must travel a quarter of the distance, and so on forever. The original distance cannot be traveled, and therefore motion is impossible.

We obviously know that motion is possible, so what is wrong with Zeno's logic? Can you find the faulty reasoning in Zeno's arguments?

ANSWER: PAGE 98

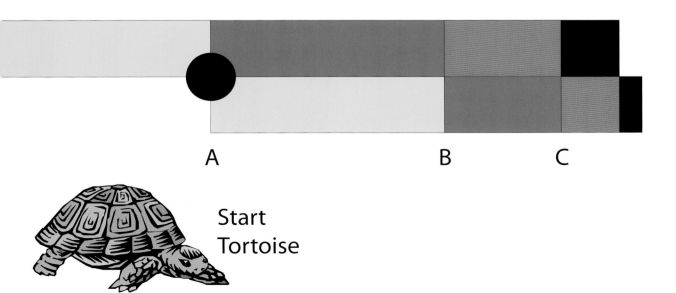

A   B   C

Start
Tortoise

▼ PEGGING HEARTS

The big heart has protruding pegs in it (represented by black dots). The three small hearts have holes as shown. Just by looking, can you see where to place the three hearts so they lie flat in the big heart, covering as many pegs as possible? Not every hole will be used on every heart. Rotating the hearts is not necessary.

ANSWER: PAGE 98

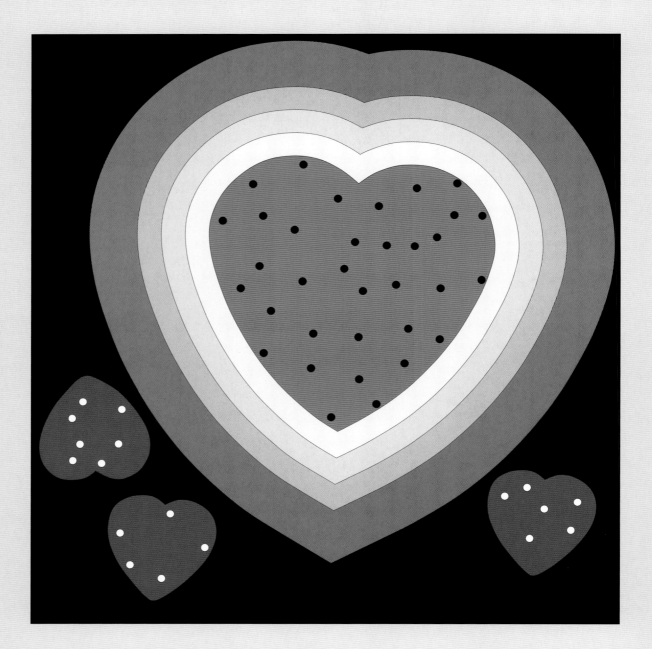

▼ WHITE BEAR

Look at the picture of the white bear, turn away, and then do your best not to think about the white bear anymore, for as long as you can.

How long will it take before the white bear pops up again in your thoughts—or, in other words, how well can you control your mind?

ANSWER: PAGE 99

Everybody knows the phrase "a picture paints a thousand words." Now you can take that concept one stage further and solve a math question too.

▼ SQUARE ROOT

Given a line of length a and another line with a length of 1 unit, draw a line x whose length is the square root of a. Can you solve the problem graphically?

ANSWER: PAGE 99

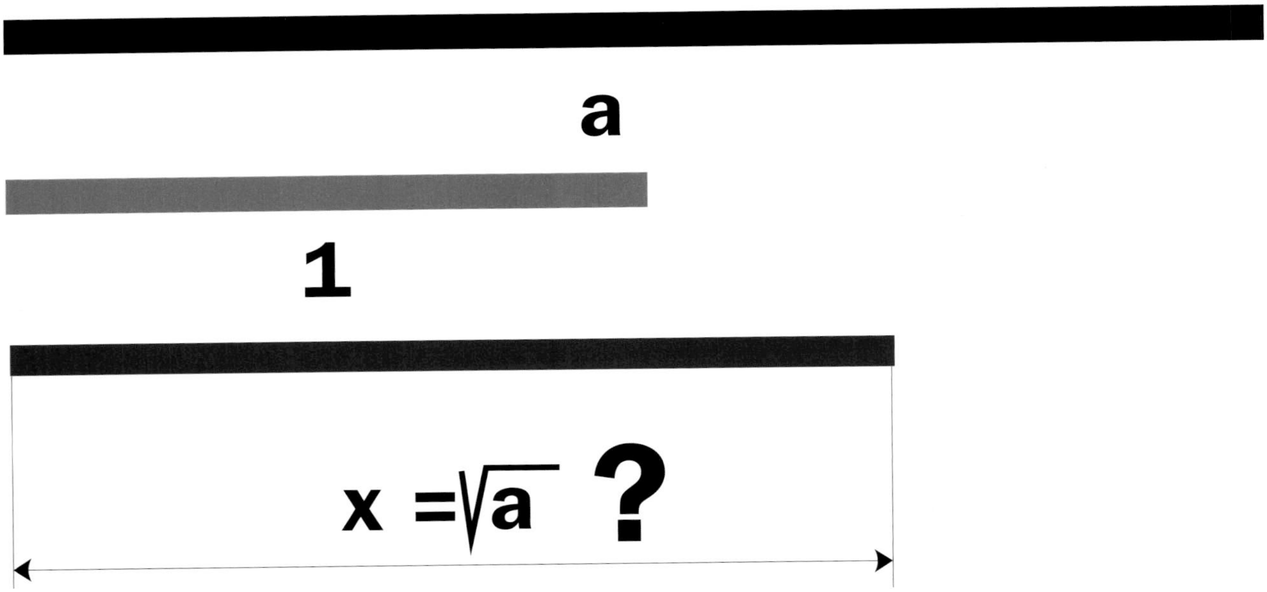

a

1

$$x = \sqrt{a} \ \ ?$$

▲ ANT PROCESSIONS

Dennis E. Shasha, a professor of computer science at New York University, defined a sequence of symbols as being "surprising" if, for every pair of symbols X and Y and every distance D, there is, at most, one position in the sequence where X precedes Y by distance D.

In our puzzle, the symbols are ants carrying eggs of different colors. Can you tell which of the six ant processions are surprising and which are not?

ANSWER: PAGE 99

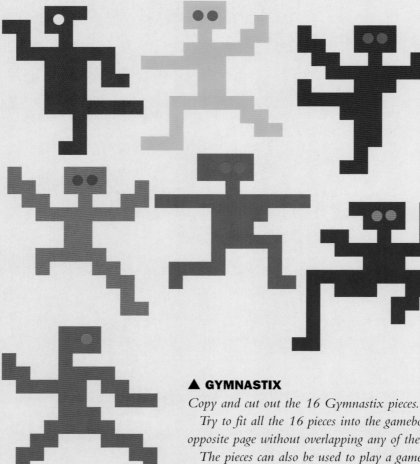

▲ GYMNASTIX

Copy and cut out the 16 Gymnastix pieces.

Try to fit all the 16 pieces into the gameboard on the opposite page without overlapping any of the pieces.

The pieces can also be used to play a game; players take turns playing a piece on the gameboard. The first player unable to place a piece is the loser.

This is a tricky puzzle, so I'll give you a hint: the Weightlifter is carrying everyone else.

ANSWER: PAGE 100

The Weightlifter

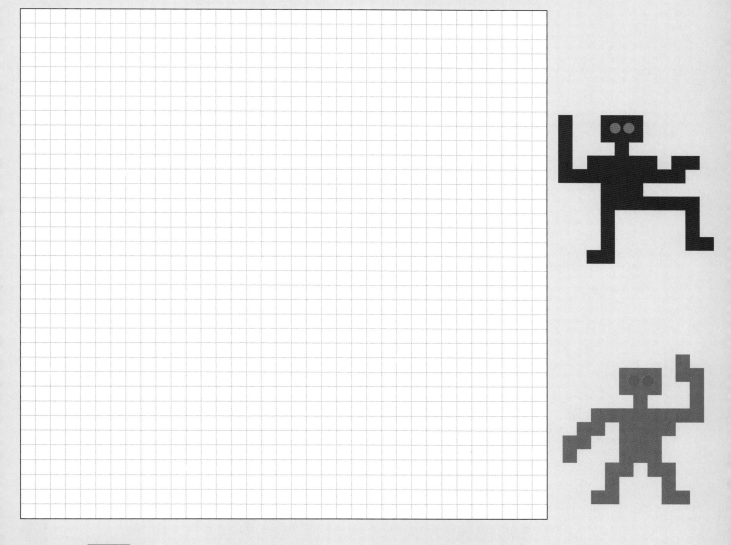

▼ COUNTING DOTS

How long will it take you to count the dots in the two square patterns?
Can you count the dots in less than 30 seconds?

ANSWER: PAGE 100

Puzzle 1

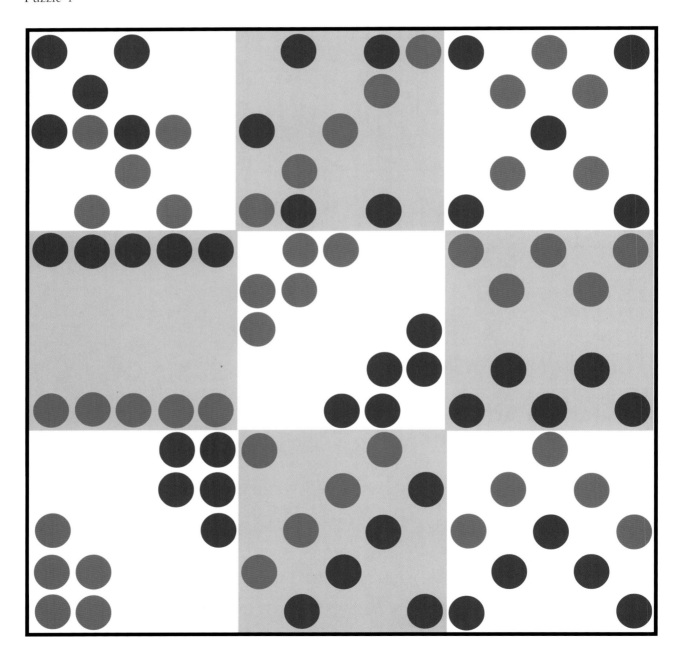

Puzzle 2

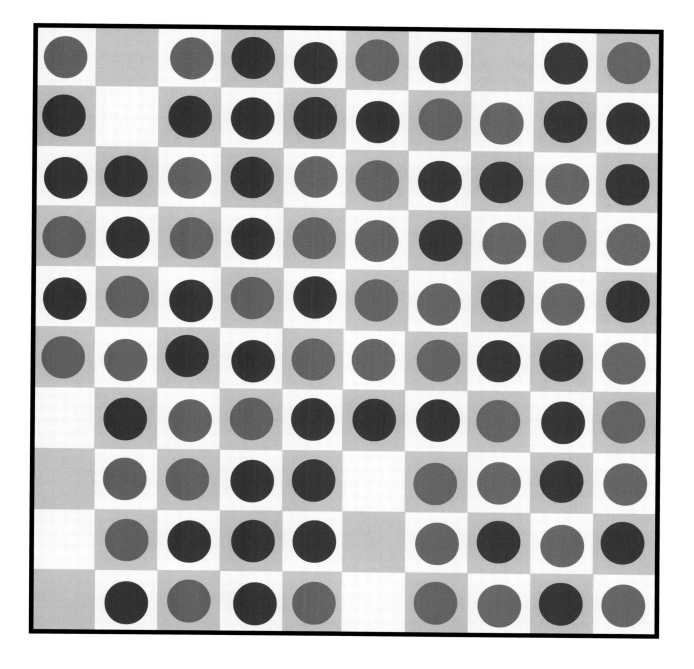

Polyominoes use the concept of dominoes and take it several steps further.

The first 8 polyominoes

▶ FIRST EIGHT POLYOMINOES

The first eight polyominoes are shown above: one domino, two trominoes, and five tetrominoes.

Puzzle 1: *The five tetrominoes (colored black and green) have a total area of 20 unit squares. Can they be fitted into a 4-by-5 rectangle?*

Puzzle 2: *The first eight polyominoes have a total area of 28 unit squares. Can they all be fitted into a 4-by-7 rectangle?*

ANSWER: PAGE 101

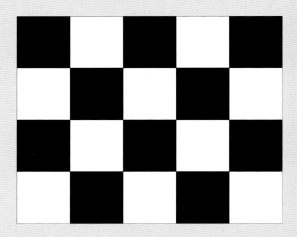

Puzzle 1

Puzzle 2

✳ Polyforms and Polyominoes

Dominoes, the familiar playing pieces of the centuries-old game, are made up of two unit squares joined fully along a common edge. Two identical squares can fit together in only one way.

But mathematicians—recreational and otherwise—have elaborated on the basic domino shape by adding more unit squares. The results—three-square trominoes, four-square tetrominoes, five-square pentominoes, and the like—are collectively known as polyominoes.

The first polyomino problem appeared in 1907, but the popularity of these shapes, both as a form of mathematical recreation, and as an educational tool, owes much to Dr. Solomon Golomb, who invented them, and to Martin Gardner, who introduced them to a wider audience.

When this principle of creating polyominoes is extended to joining other identical polygons besides squares, we get polyforms.

Many books and puzzles have been published that involve polyforms, polyominoes, and especially pentominoes. The computer game Tetris uses a set of tetrominoes. Included here are a few classic and new problems involving polyominoes.

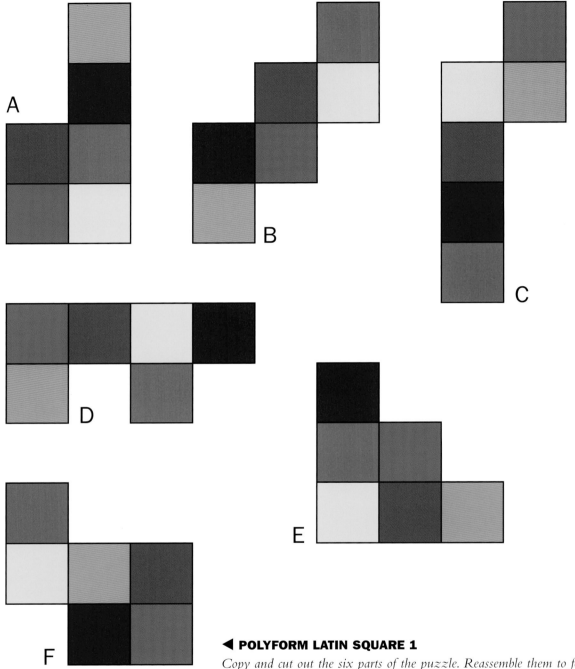

◀ POLYFORM LATIN SQUARE 1

Copy and cut out the six parts of the puzzle. Reassemble them to form a square in which every horizontal row and vertical column contains squares of six different colors, called a Latin Square.

For a harder challenge, try solving the puzzle in your head, without cutting out the pieces.

ANSWER: PAGE 101

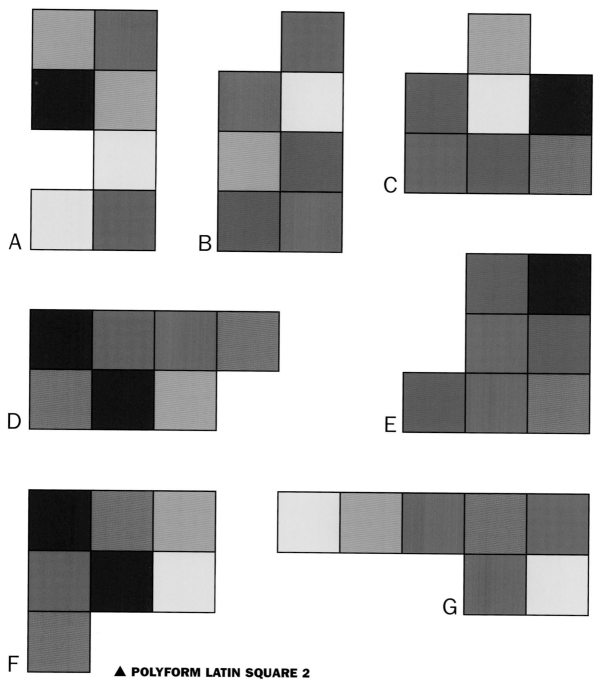

▲ POLYFORM LATIN SQUARE 2

Copy and cut out the seven parts of the puzzle.

Reassemble them to form a Latin square, in which every horizontal row and vertical column contains squares of seven different colors.

For a harder challenge, try solving the puzzle in your head, without cutting out the pieces.

ANSWER: PAGE 102

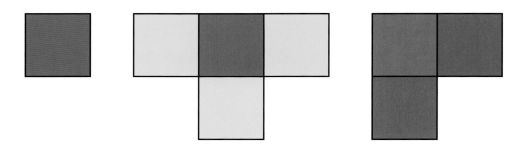

▲ POLYOMINO SYMMETRY

Copy the monomino, T-tetromino, and L-tromino; cut them out; and put them together to create symmetrical shapes, as shown in the example below.

How many shapes can you create which have either reflective or rotational symmetry? There are 17 such symmetrical shapes—perhaps more than you would expect. We have shown where the monomino is placed in the other 16 shapes; can you complete them?

Note: the colors do not matter when creating the symmetry.

ANSWER: PAGE **102**

The line of symmetry

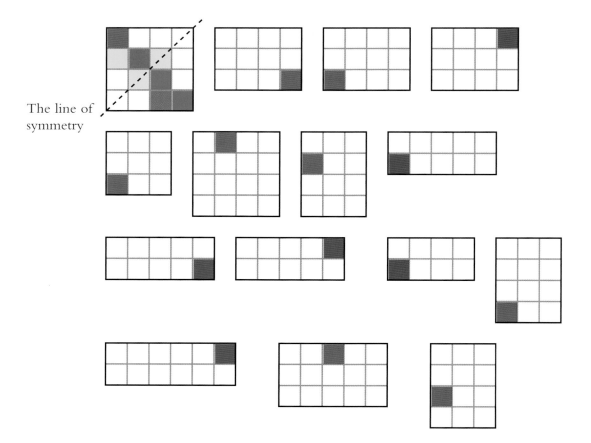

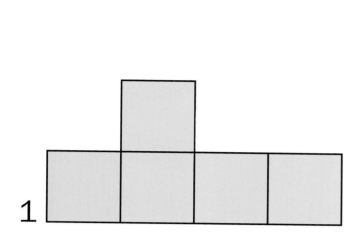

1

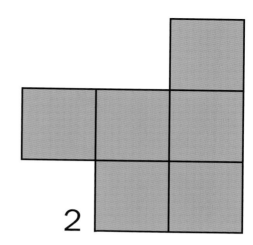

2

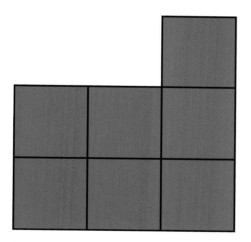

3

POLYOMINO TILING RECTANGLES

David Klarner defined the order of a polyomino as the smallest number of congruent copies of the polyomino which can be put together to form a rectangle. Rotations and reflections of the polyomino are allowed.

From the above definition, a polyomino of order 1 is itself a rectangle.

Can you find the order for each of the polyominoes shown here?

ANSWER: PAGE 103

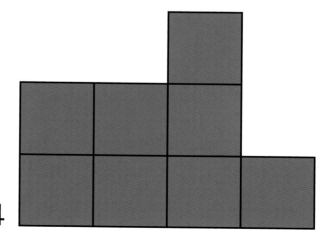

4

Step-by-Step uses monominoes, dominoes, and straight trominoes as pieces for a puzzle and for a two-person strategy game. Fitting the pieces together looks simple but requires you to think ahead!

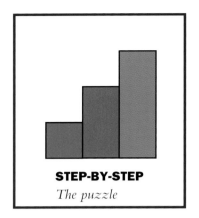

STEP-BY-STEP
The puzzle

▶STEP-BY-STEP
THE PUZZLE

By joining a monomino, a domino, and a straight tromino, how many different configurations can you create according to the following rules and restrictions:

1) The orientation of the pieces must stay vertical.

2) The shorter of two adjacent pieces may not extend past the edge of the longer piece (see example, right).

3) Mirror reversals are considered to be different.

4) Pieces must line up along an imaginary grid with squares the size of the monomino.

5) All three pieces must stay connected.

ANSWER: PAGE 103

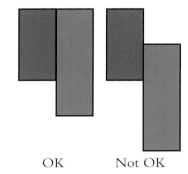

OK   Not OK

▶STEP-BY-STEP
THE GAME

A two-person strategy game played with a set of a monomino, domino, and tromino for each player.

Players take turns placing their shapes on a 4-by-4 gameboard in sequence, first the monomino, then the domino, then the tromino. When all the pieces have been placed, successive moves follow the same order by repositioning the pieces already on the board.

The winner of the game is the first player who succeeds in creating a staircase configuration of his or her color, which can be in any orientation on the gameboard.

A player must make a move on every turn; a player may not pass or replace a piece in the same position. It is also illegal to make a move which makes it impossible for the other player to move.

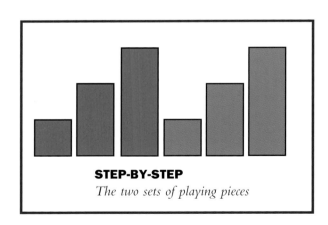

STEP-BY-STEP
The two sets of playing pieces

STEP-BY-STEP
The winning position

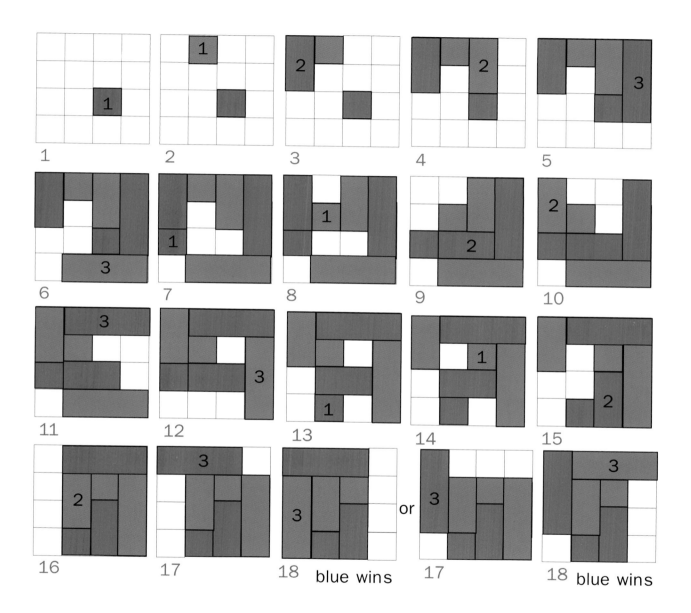

▲ **STEP-BY-STEP**

A sample game in which the blue player forces a win on the 18th move.

▲ TWELVE PENTOMINOES

The twelve pentominoes are shown above.

Can you fit them all into the grid opposite, leaving only the four black squares uncovered? Rotating and flipping pieces is allowed.

ANSWER: PAGE 104

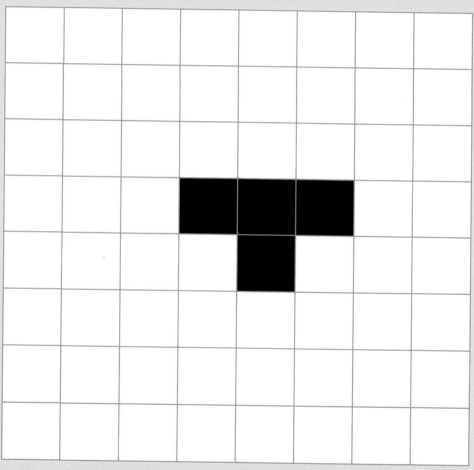

The grid

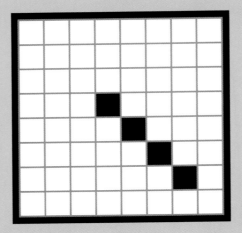

Puzzle 1

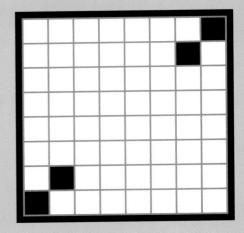

Puzzle 2

▶ **PENTOMINO PUZZLES**

Can you fit the set of 12 pentominoes in the six puzzle boards, leaving the four black squares uncovered? Note that reflections and rotations of the pieces are allowed.

ANSWER: PAGE 104

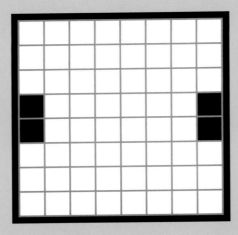

Puzzle 3

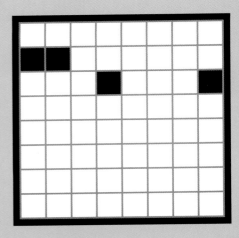

Puzzle 4

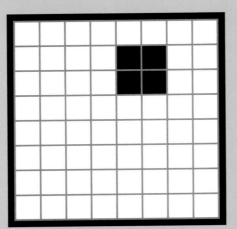

Puzzle 5

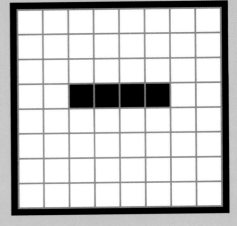

Puzzle 6

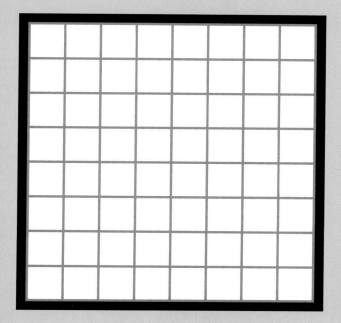

◄ MINIMAL PENTOMINO PUZZLE

What is the smallest number of pentominoes which can be placed on the 8-by-8 gameboard to make it impossible for any further pentominoes to be placed on the board?

ANSWER: PAGE 105

▲ PENTOMINO TRISECTIONS

Can you draw the outlines of three pentominoes in each grid?
Each of the 12 pentominoes should be used exactly once.

ANSWER: PAGE 105

▲ PENTOMINO TRIPLICATION

A fascinating pentomino puzzle is the triplication problem. Given a pentomino piece, use nine of the other pentominoes to create a scale-model replica, three times as wide and three times as high as the original pentomino.

All the twelve pentomino pieces can be triplicated. Can you solve all of them?

ANSWER: PAGE 106

Fitting the set of 12 pentominoes into the provided shapes is more difficult than it seems. Make sure that none of the shapes overlap the space of another.

▼ PENTOMINO FENCE 1
The Maximum Rectangle Fence

The largest rectangular enclosure which can be surrounded by a rectangular fence using the set of 12 pentominoes is shown.

Can you find the outlines of the pentominoes forming the fence?

ANSWER: PAGE 107

Enclosure:
28 unit squares

▼ **PENTOMINO FENCE 2**

The Maximum Rectangle Enclosure

The largest rectangular enclosure that can be formed by the set of 12 pentominoes is a 9-by-10 rectangle and has an area of 90 unit squares.

Can you find the outlines of the pentominoes forming the fence?

ANSWER: PAGE 107

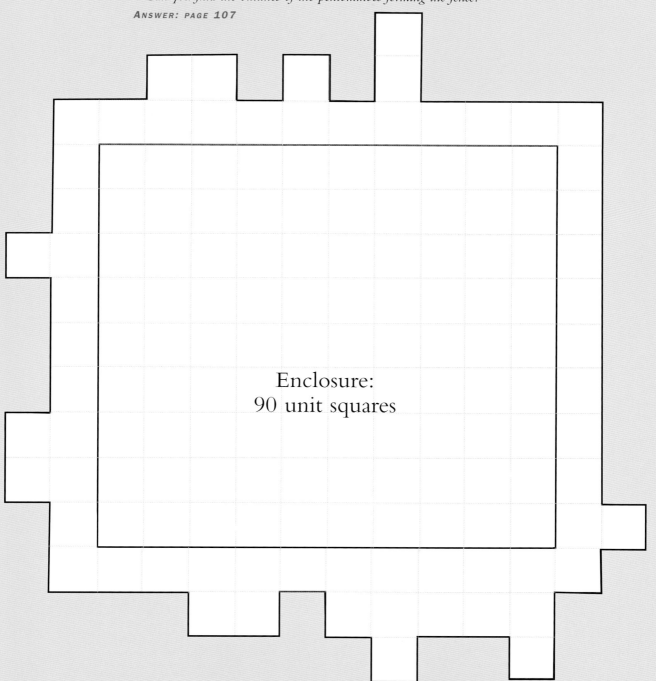

Enclosure:
90 unit squares

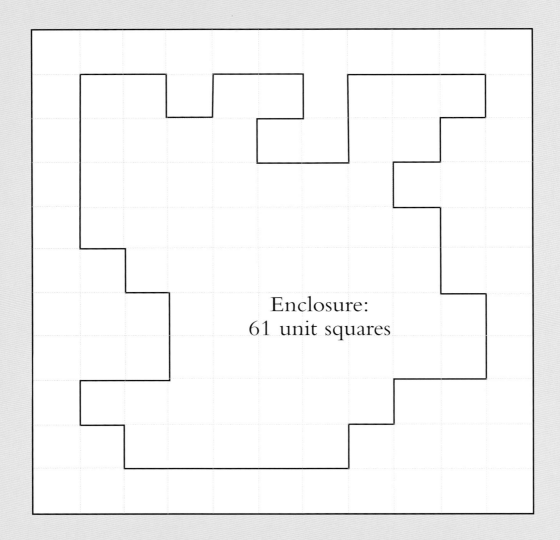

Enclosure:
61 unit squares

▲ PENTOMINO FENCE 3

The Maximum Rectangular Fence

The largest rectangular fence surrounding an enclosure of any shape that can be made from pentominoes is an 11-by-11 square enclosing an area of 61 unit squares.

Can you find the outlines of the individual pentominoes forming the fence?

ANSWER: PAGE 107

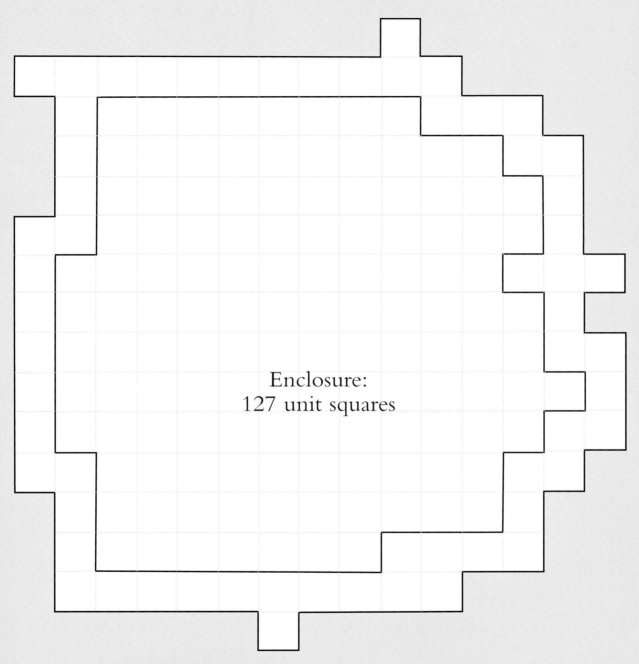

Enclosure:
127 unit squares

▲ PENTOMINO FENCE 4
The Maximum Enclosure Problem

The largest enclosure of any shape that can be made from the set of 12 pentominoes has an area of 127 unit squares.

Can you find the outlines of the pentominoes forming the fence?

ANSWER: PAGE 107

▲ JAGGED EDGE PENTOMINO PUZZLE 1

Here we have two polygonal gameboards with jagged edges, on which the pentominoes can be arranged diagonally.

Can you cover each board with the set of 12 pentominoes from page 24? (There will be one empty square left over on each board.)

ANSWER: PAGE **108**

▲ JAGGED EDGE PENTOMINO PUZZLE 2

ANSWER: PAGE 108

What you have learned so far about how polyominoes fit together will help when it comes to fitting the missing pieces into this polyomino jigsaw puzzle.

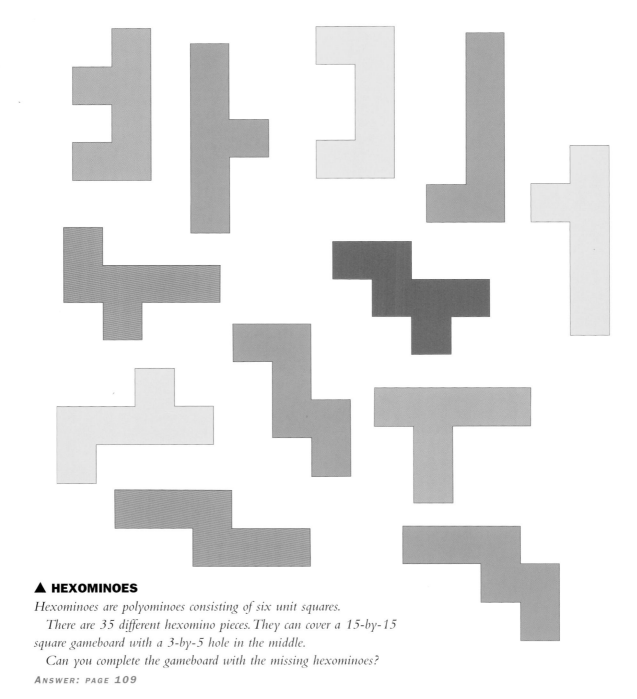

▲ HEXOMINOES

Hexominoes are polyominoes consisting of six unit squares.

There are 35 different hexomino pieces. They can cover a 15-by-15 square gameboard with a 3-by-5 hole in the middle.

Can you complete the gameboard with the missing hexominoes?

ANSWER: PAGE 109

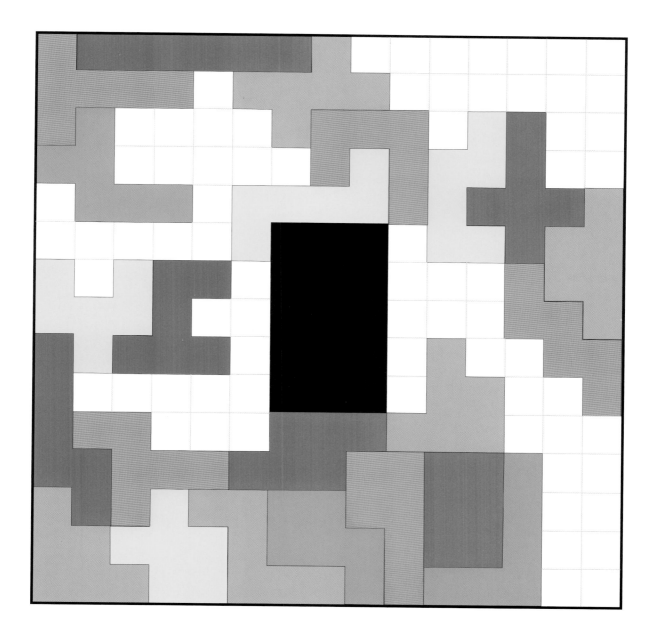

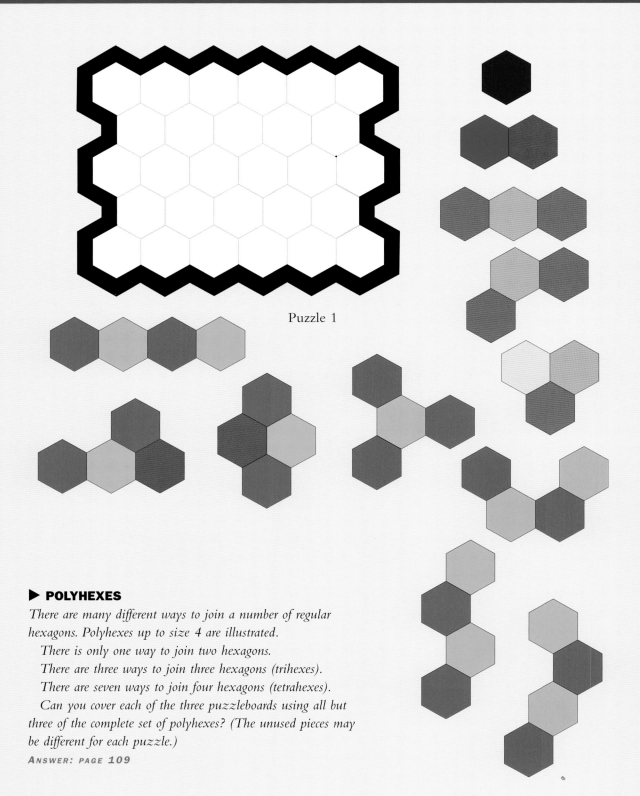

Puzzle 1

▶ POLYHEXES

There are many different ways to join a number of regular hexagons. Polyhexes up to size 4 are illustrated.

There is only one way to join two hexagons.

There are three ways to join three hexagons (trihexes).

There are seven ways to join four hexagons (tetrahexes).

Can you cover each of the three puzzleboards using all but three of the complete set of polyhexes? (The unused pieces may be different for each puzzle.)

ANSWER: PAGE 109

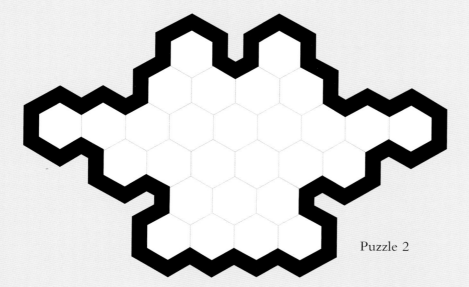

Puzzle 2

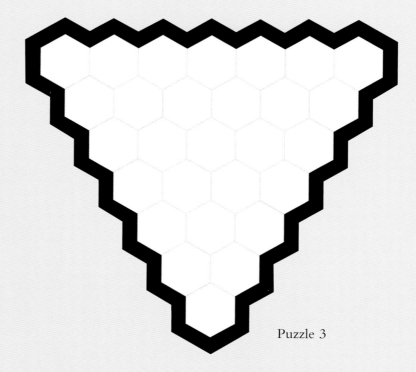

Puzzle 3

▼ PENTAHEXES

There are 22 possible distinct pentahexes. Each one has five hexagons joined along their sides.

The Puzzle: *Can you fit the complete set of pentahexes on the gameboard?*

ANSWER: PAGE 110

The Game: *Two players take turns placing a pentahex on the board. The first player unable to place a pentahex is the loser.*

The pentahex gameboard

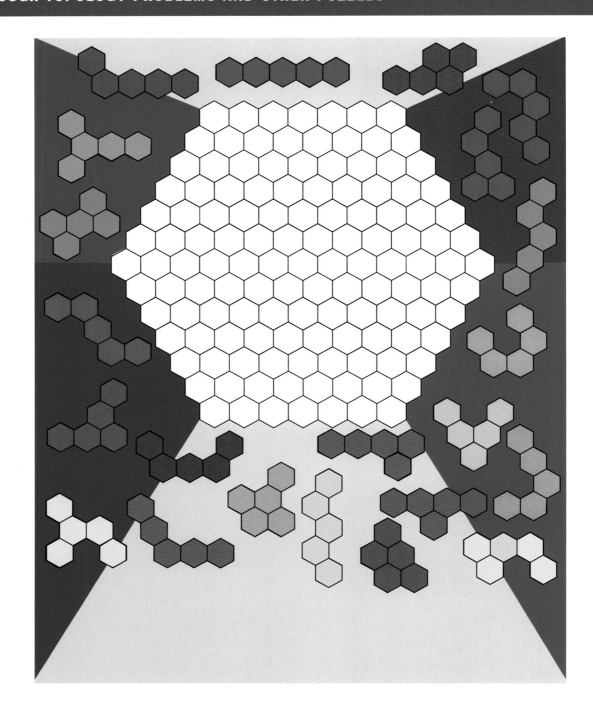

▲ PENTAHEX GAME

Using the 22 pentahexes, a two-player game can be played on a hexagonal gameboard, inspired by the famous "Hex" game invented by Piet Hein. Players alternate moves to be the first to create a continuous chain of pentahexes connecting two identically colored outlines on the gameboard.

The pieces are mutually shared by the players, and the winner is the first to connect any two identically colored areas at the side of the board, e.g. creating a path of pentahexes from blue to blue or green to green.

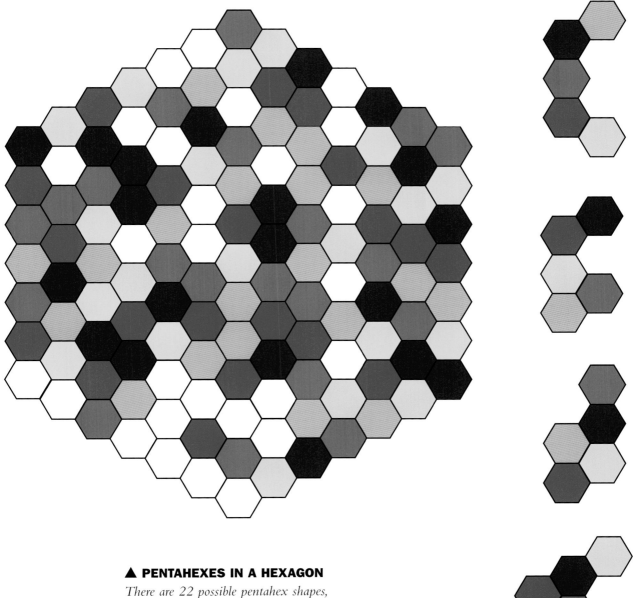

▲ PENTAHEXES IN A HEXAGON

There are 22 possible pentahex shapes, a number of which were used to form the pattern shown above.

Can you tell which of the four pentahexes shown on the right-hand side of the page were not used to form the pattern?

ANSWER: PAGE 110

Turn back to page 40 to find the complete set of 22 pentahexes. You'll need them for the puzzles below.

▶ **PENTAHEXES DOUBLE PUZZLE**

Can you cover the two grids using the complete set of 22 pentahexes?

ANSWER: PAGE *110*

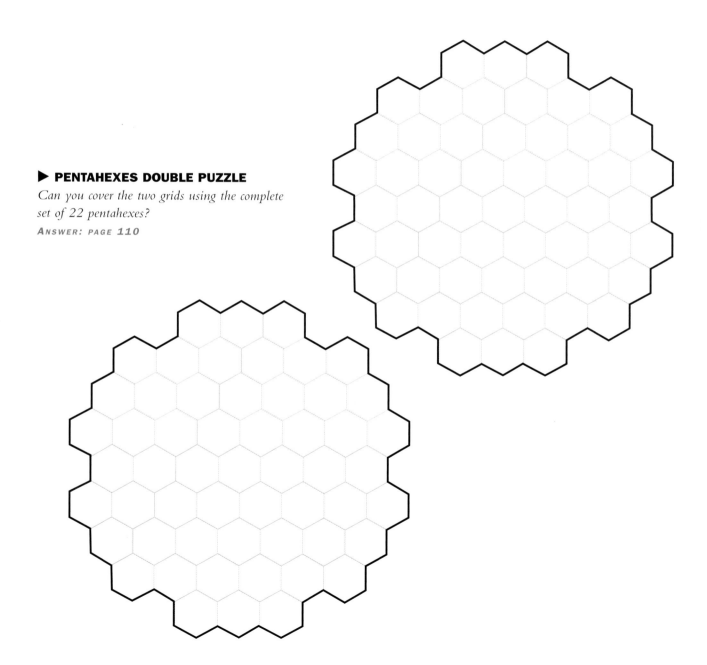

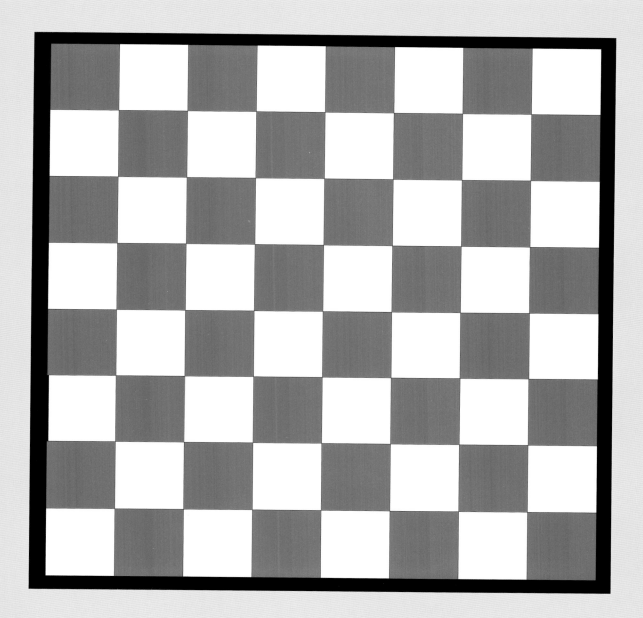

▲ CHESSBOARD SQUARES

How many squares of different sizes can you find along the grid of a chessboard? Offhand, you might say there are 64 squares. But there are larger squares than the 64 unit squares in the square matrix.

Can you find the total number of squares of different sizes?

Can you generalize a way to find the number of squares of different sizes that there are in a square grid with n *unit squares on a side?*

ANSWER: PAGE 111

To keep things interesting, let's move on from squares and hexagons to triangles. Hexiamonds are triangular counterparts of polyominoes, created by joining six identical equilateral triangles together.

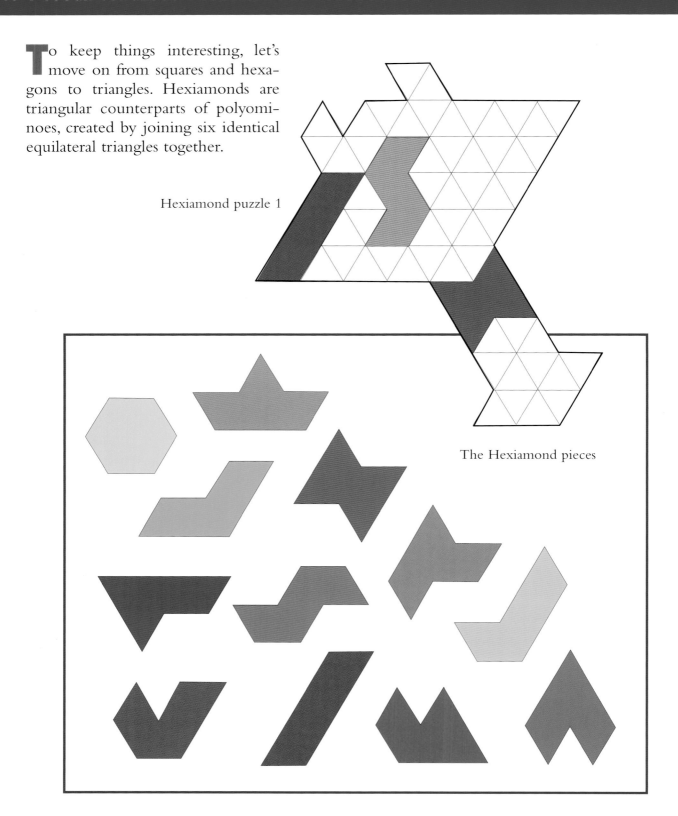

Hexiamond puzzle 1

The Hexiamond pieces

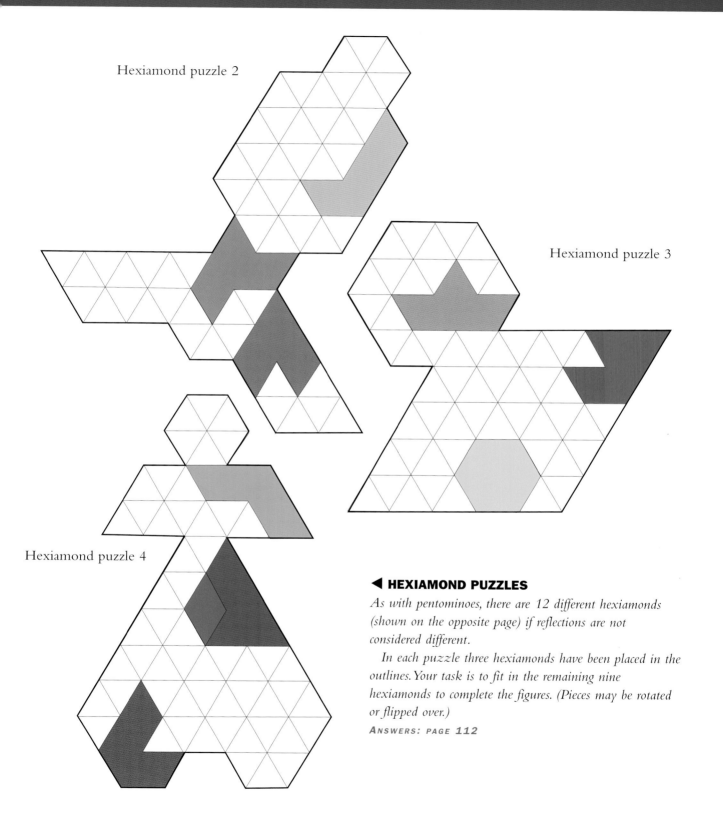

Hexiamond puzzle 2

Hexiamond puzzle 3

Hexiamond puzzle 4

◄ HEXIAMOND PUZZLES

As with pentominoes, there are 12 different hexiamonds (shown on the opposite page) if reflections are not considered different.

In each puzzle three hexiamonds have been placed in the outlines. Your task is to fit in the remaining nine hexiamonds to complete the figures. (Pieces may be rotated or flipped over.)

ANSWERS: PAGE 112

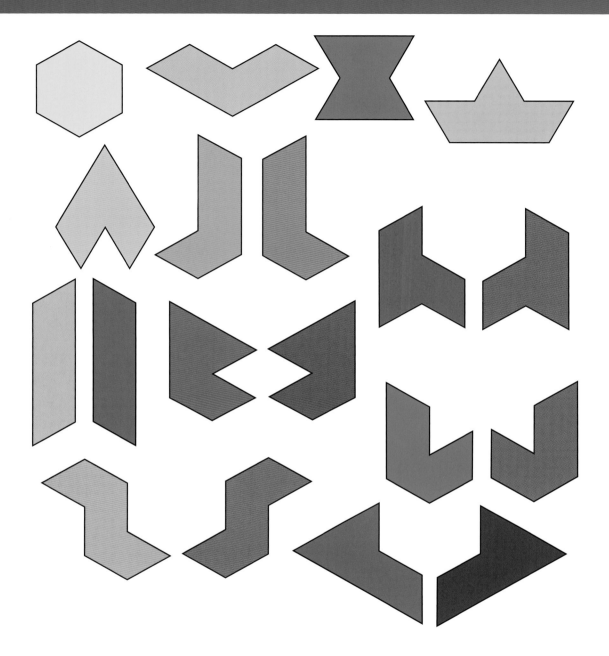

▲ HEXIAMONDS OF O'BEIRNE

In 1959, Thomas H. O'Beirne noticed that among the polyominoes which can be formed by joining six equilateral triangles, five are symmetrical while seven are not.

If we count the reflections of the asymmetrical hexiamonds as unique pieces, we get a set of 19 shapes which together have the same area as a gameboard consisting of a 3-by-3

configuration of regular hexagons. O'Beirne posed the challenging problem:

Can the 19 shapes cover the gameboard of 19 regular hexagons? His problem is one of the most challenging two-dimensional puzzles. It took O'Beirne several months to find a solution. Can you find one?

ANSWER: PAGE 112

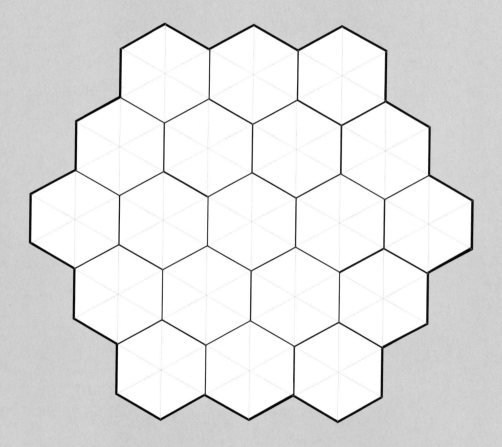

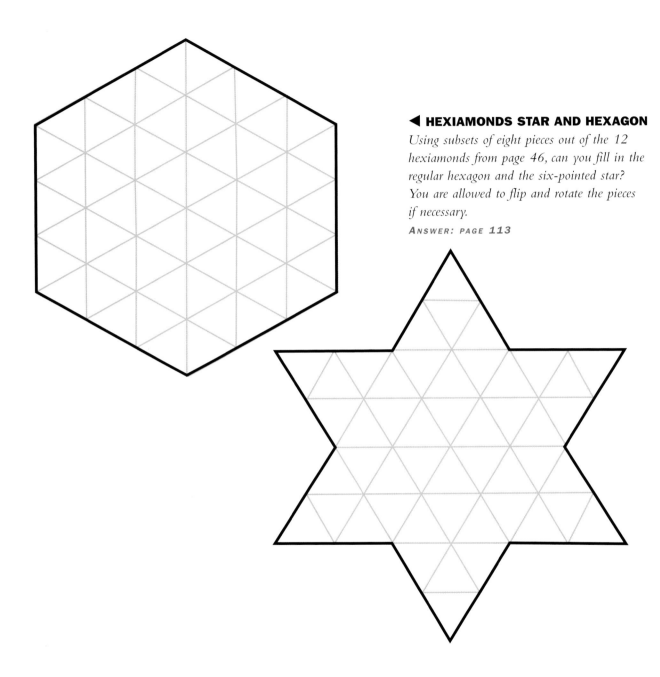

◀ HEXIAMONDS STAR AND HEXAGON

Using subsets of eight pieces out of the 12 hexiamonds from page 46, can you fill in the regular hexagon and the six-pointed star? You are allowed to flip and rotate the pieces if necessary.

ANSWER: PAGE 113

▲ HEPTIAMONDS

There are 24 heptiamonds, made by combining seven equilateral triangles.
Thomas O'Beirne proposed the problem of finding which heptiamonds
can tessellate the plane (that is to say, which pieces could tile an infinitely
large floor using multiple copies of that shape without leaving any gaps).
Gregory J. Bishop proved that only one cannot.

Can you find it?

ANSWER: PAGE 114

Thomas O'Beirne's next set of polyaboloes takes the idea of combining shapes further, this time by using isosceles triangles.

▼TETRABOLO SQUARE

This square can be covered with the eight tetraboloes that do not possess horizontal or vertical symmetry plus their mirror images—16 pieces in all.

Can you figure out how?

ANSWER: PAGE **114**

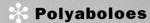

❋ Polyaboloes

We can also join together polygonal units that are not regular. Polyaboloes are right-angled isosceles triangles joined together either along their sides or along their hypotenuses.

There are 3 diaboloes, 4 triaboloes, and 14 tetraboloes.

They were first described in 1961 by Thomas H. O'Beirne.

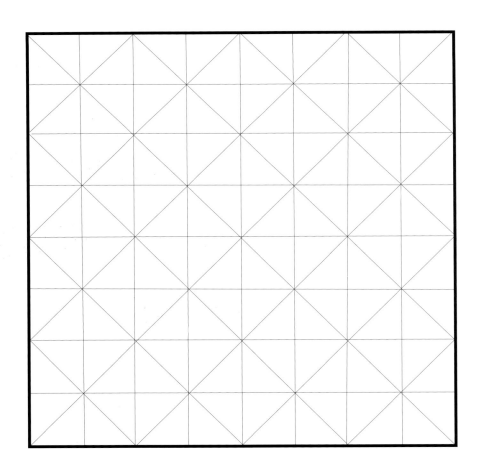

Polyaboloes: the 3 diaboloes,
4 triaboloes, and 14 tetraboloes.

▲ FISHNET

Can you fit all 18 fish into the fishnet?

ANSWER: PAGE 115

❈ Reptiles

Did you know that some shapes, if they are combined with a specific number of identical shapes of the same size, can create larger versions of themselves? And, correspondingly, that when such shapes are subdivided appropriately, they also can make smaller versions of themselves?

These polygons that can make larger and smaller copies of themselves are called "reptiles."

Solomon Golomb gave them their name and by studying them laid the groundwork for a general theory of polygon replication.

▲ MONUMENT

The monument was built from a number of identical smaller shapes, each one an exact replica of the larger monument. Can you find the number of the smaller building blocks and their orientation along the grid lines?

ANSWER: PAGE 115

Sometimes things are not as they appear. There are many illusions which rely on the brain tricking the eye into seeing what isn't really there. Here the trick is to spot the lines that aren't parallel.

▲ PARALLELS

One classic illusion is the "Zollner Illusion," devised by the psychologist Johann Zollner (1834–1882), in which a set of parallel lines don't look parallel, because of the distorting effect of the background lines intersecting the parallel lines at acute angles (10–30 degrees).

Our illusion is a slightly modified version of Zollner's. Some lines are parallel, some are not. Can you tell which are which?

ANSWER: PAGE **116**

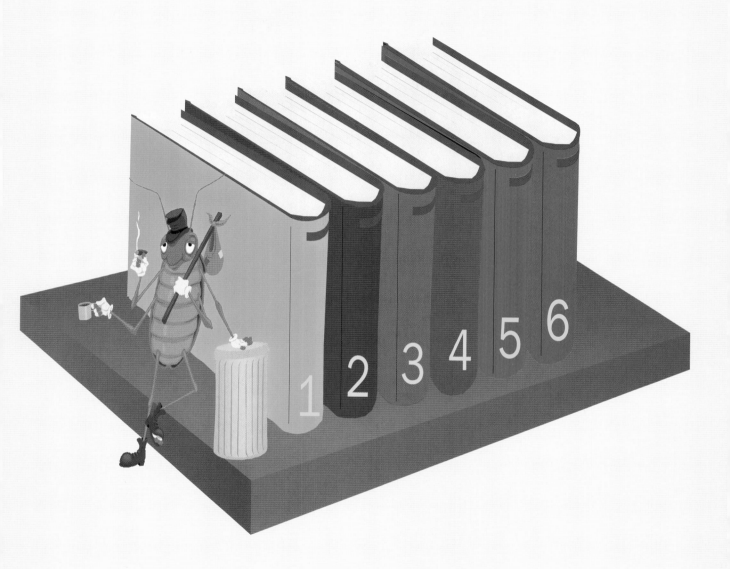

▲ BOOKWORM

The hungry bookworm eats his way through six volumes. He eats straight through from the first page of volume one to the last page of volume six. What is the distance the worm covered in the course of accomplishing this feat?

Note: Each volume is six centimeters thick, including the covers, which are each half a centimeter thick.

ANSWER: PAGE 116

Map coloring can be a tricky business. Making sure that two areas with a shared border are shaded two different colors is important. But the big question is, how many colors does a mapmaker need? You'll be surprised.

▲ COLORING MAPS

How many colors are needed to color the three maps so that no two regions with a common border have the same color?

ANSWER: PAGE 116

▲ FOUR-COLOR HEXAGONS GAME

This is a coloring game for two players using four colors: yellow, green, blue, and red.

Players take turns choosing a hexagon adjacent to a hexagon already colored, coloring it with one of the four available colors. Adjacent hexagons may not be the same color. Additionally, hexagons along the border may not be the same color as any border region or region it touches.

The player who makes the last legal move is the winner.

As a solitaire puzzle, can you fully color all the hexagons of the gameboard according to the above rules?

ANSWER: PAGE 117

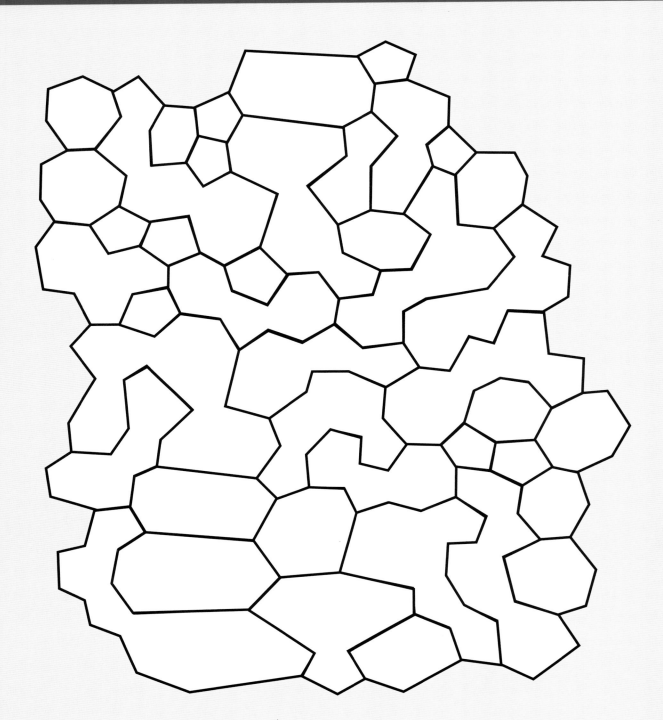

▲ COLORING PATTERN

Color the pattern so that no two regions with a common border are the same color.

How many colors are needed?

ANSWER: PAGE 117

▲ GRAPH COLORING

How many colors are needed to color each region so that no two adjacent regions have the same color?

ANSWER: PAGE 117

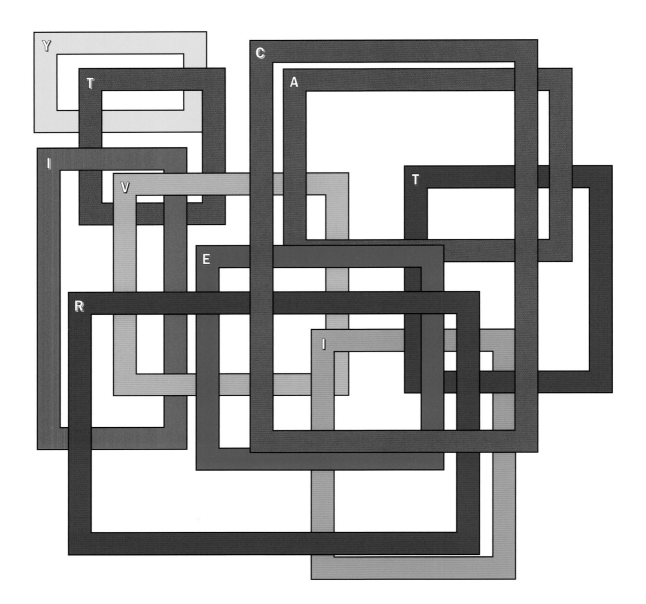

▲ LIFT OFF

Each of these frames can be lifted off the pile one at a time so that none of them disturbs any other.

In your mind's eye, can you find the correct order in which to pick them up?

When you have solved the puzzle, the letters on the frames (read in the order you picked them up) will spell out an appropriate word.

ANSWER: PAGE *118*

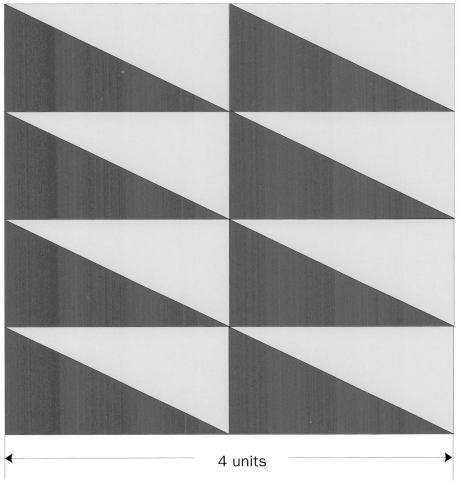

4 units

▲ TRIANGLES IN A SQUARE

The sides of the right-angled triangles are 1 and 2 units. Sixteen such triangles can form a 4-by-4 square as shown.

Can you make a square using 20 identical triangles of the same proportions?

How about 80?

ANSWER: PAGE 118

▼ PAPER PENTAGON

It's well-known that you can tie a knot in a strip of paper and create a perfect pentagon as shown.

If you join the two ends, a closed surface is obtained. Can you tell how many sides and edges this surface will have?

ANSWER: PAGE 118

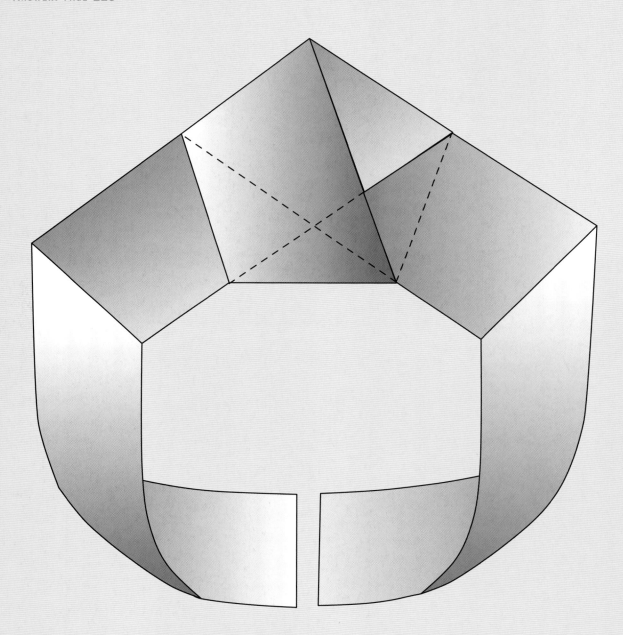

▲ DOUBLE TOWERS

How many moves are needed to change the five blocks of the sliding block puzzle at the top into the two towers of the bottom block? (The gray space is the empty space.)

ANSWER: PAGE 118

MAZES

Mazes are ancient structures. Legend has it that the first maze was built by Daedalus for King Minos of Crete to house the Minotaur, a monster that was half bull, half man. Theseus went into the labyrinth to kill the Minotaur and found his way back by using a ball of golden thread that he unspooled on the way in.

From a mathematical standpoint, a maze is a problem in topology. A maze can be solved quickly on paper by shading all the blind alleys until only the right route remains. But when you do not possess a map of the maze and you are inside it, there are still algorithms that can be used to find the exit. For instance, a maze can be easily solved by placing your hand

This circular maze is one of the oldest labyrinth designs.

against the right (or left) wall and keeping it there as you walk. If you do this, you are sure to reach the exit eventually, though your route may not be the shortest one. This method will not work, however, with mazes in which the goal is within the labyrinth and surrounded by closed circuits (detached walls).

Mazes that contain no closed circuits are called simply connected—that is, they have no detached walls. Mazes with detached walls are sure to contain closed circuits, and are called multiply connected, as shown on this page.

There is a mechanical procedure which solves all mazes:

As you walk through the maze, draw a line on one side of the path, say, your right. When you come to a new juncture of paths, take any path you wish. If you later return to a previously visited juncture, turn around and go back the way you came.

If, in the course of walking along an old path (a path marked on your left), you come to a previously visited juncture, take any new path if one is available; otherwise take an old path. Never enter a path marked on both sides.

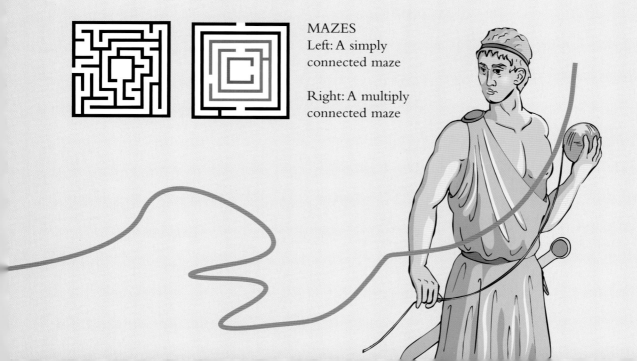

MAZES
Left: A simply connected maze

Right: A multiply connected maze

▶ CUMAZE

Photocopy and cut out the diagram, and fold it into a cube, then try to get from 1 to 2. How quickly can you do it?

ANSWER: PAGE 119

in

out

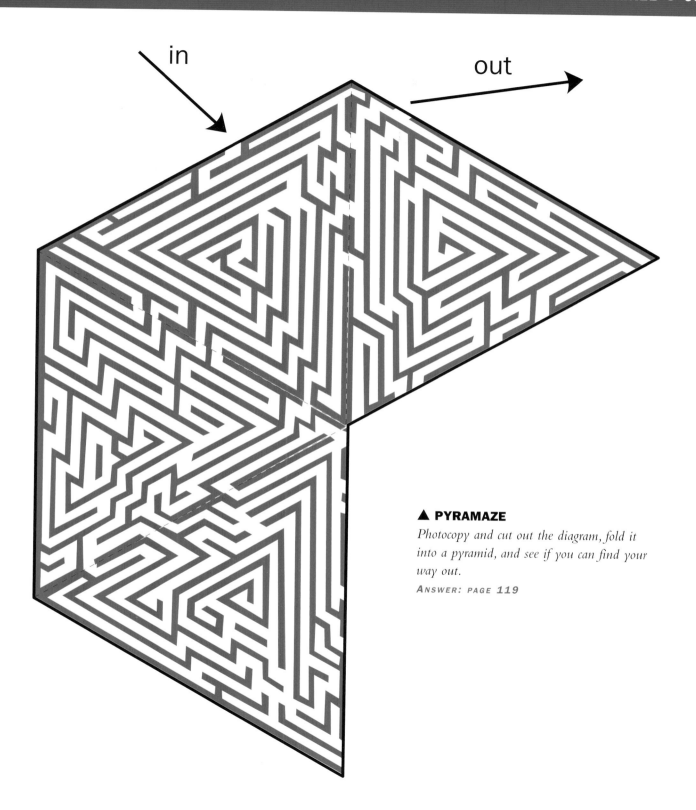

▲ PYRAMAZE

Photocopy and cut out the diagram, fold it into a pyramid, and see if you can find your way out.

ANSWER: PAGE 119

▼ CARROLL'S MAZE

Starting in the central diamond, can you find your way out of the maze?
(Note that the paths weave over and under each other.)

ANSWER: PAGE 119

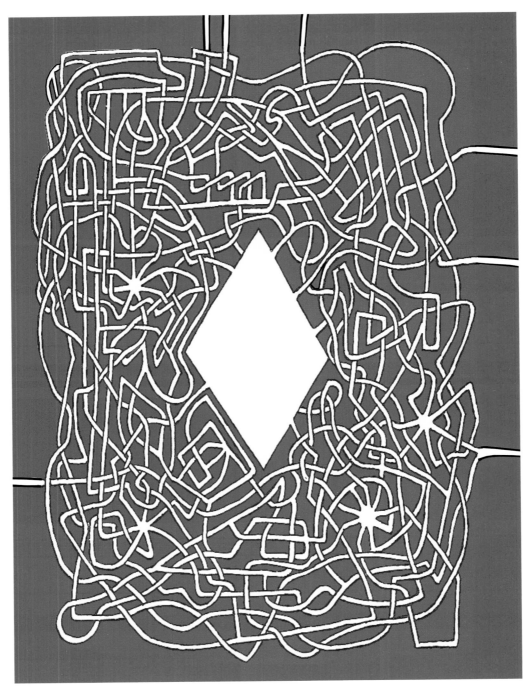

▲ **HEX-MAZE**

Can you find the shortest path to traverse the honeycomb?

ANSWER: PAGE 120

Ⓗ ow many ways are there to fold a square? This simple idea forms the basis of these next two puzzles. But there is more to it than that, as sequences and shapes form part of the question.

▼ MISSING SQUARES

Can you fill in the missing square in each horizontal row of the 16-square series?

ANSWER: PAGE 120

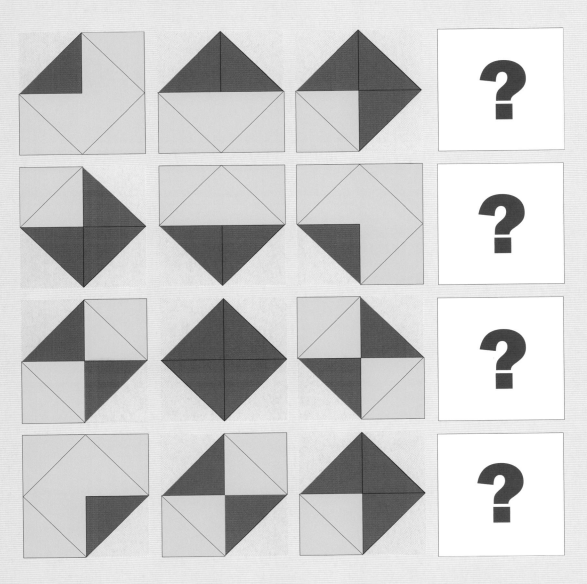

1) Folding to join two opposite corners (vertices) gives a diagonal, which cuts the square into two congruent (equal) right-angled isosceles triangles.

2) Folding the other two opposite corners of the square gives the second diagonal, meeting the first in a point at the center of the square, dividing it into four congruent (equal) right-angled isosceles triangles.

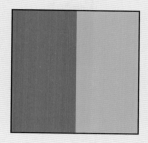

3) We can halve the square another way, by folding the two opposite sides, thus bisecting the square by a line parallel to the two sides, resulting in two congruent rectangles.

4) We can also quarter the square another way, by further folding the two sides, which gives us four congruent squares. The two bisecting lines go through the center of the square.

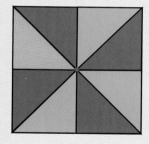

5) With all four folds together, we can demonstrate the axes of symmetry of the square. There are four axes of reflectional symmetry; additionally, the square has rotational symmetry around the center point.

▲ SQUARE FOLD

In geometry, the square is a rectilinear figure of four equal sides and four right angles. Or, to put it another way: a square is a rectangle all of whose sides are congruent.

Just by folding a square piece of paper, and without using any other tools, you can obtain a great variety of interesting mathematical results. A simple sequence of folds is demonstrated, resulting in a surprising number of mathematical discoveries.

1) Can you fold a square piece of paper to obtain a series of squares in four or more different sizes?

2) Can you fold a square piece of paper into a regular octagon?

3) Can you fold a square piece of paper to get an orderly honeycomb tessellation of hexagons?

ANSWER: PAGES 120 AND 121

This sliding-block game originated in Japan, and has spawned many variations, including some that may have appeared in your Christmas stocking.

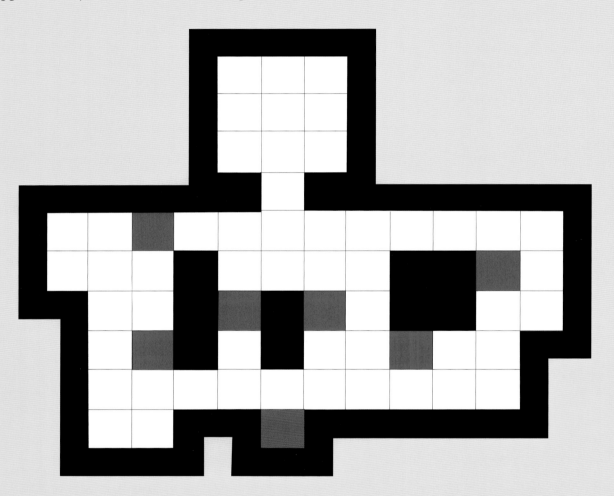

▲ SOKOBAN

A map of a warehouse is shown; crates are represented by red squares and the warehouse man is represented by a blue square.

The object is to push all the crates into the top storage space. The warehouse man can only move crates by pushing them. He can push them in any horizontal or vertical direction, but he must not move them diagonally. He can move only one crate at a time. A single push counts as one move, no matter how far the warehouse man pushes a crate. For instance, the sequence shown at right counts as two moves.

In how many moves can you solve the puzzle?

ANSWER: PAGE *122*

Crates

Sokoban, the warehouse man

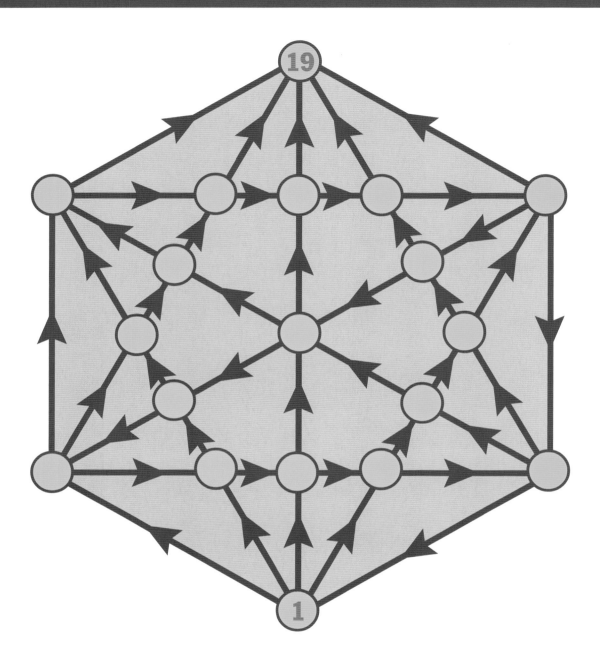

▲ HAMILTON'S PATH

Try to create a path from one circle to the next, placing the numbers from 1 to 19 sequentially on the gameboard above. You may only visit each circle once and must always travel from one circle to another in the direction of the arrow on the line that connects them.

No jumps are allowed.

ANSWER: PAGE 123

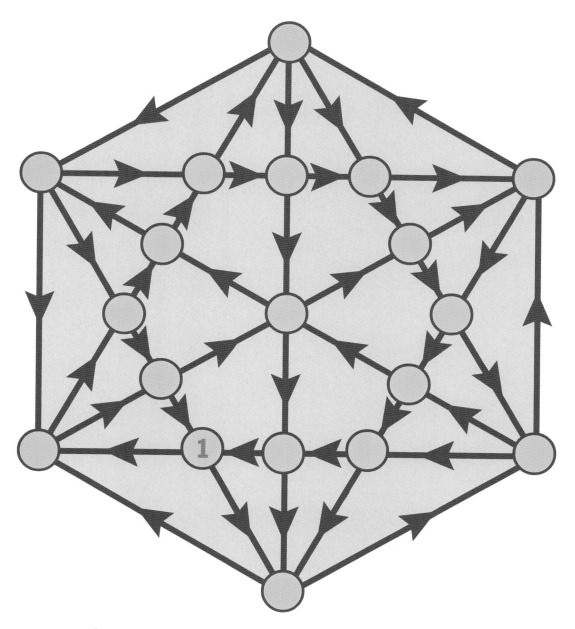

▲ HAMILTON'S LOOP

A perfect Hamiltonian circuit visits every point on a graph and returns to the point it started from, thus creating a continuous loop. Can you place the numbers from 1 to 19 sequentially on the gameboard above to create such a loop?

You may only visit each circle once and must always travel from one circle to another in the direction of the arrow on the line that connects them. No jumps are allowed.

ANSWER: PAGE *123*

Something as simple as a strip of stamps can provide the basis for various puzzles. We have used blocks of three, four, six and eight stamps to pose a series of sequencing questions.

▶ FOLDING THREE STAMPS

Just by looking, can you tell how many different ways you can fold a strip of three stamps?

You may only fold on the perforations, and the end result must be a stack of three stamps on top of each other.

It does not matter whether the stamps are face up or face down.

There are six possible permutations of three colors, as shown.

How many can you achieve by folding?

ANSWER: PAGE 124

1
2
3
4
5
6

✳ Map folding

The Polish mathematician Stanislaw Ulam was the first pose the question: In how many different ways can a map be folded? The problem has frustrated researchers in the field of modern combinatorial theory ever since. Indeed, the general problem of map folding is still unsolved.

There is an old saying that is appropriate here:

"The easiest way to fold a road map is—differently!"

▲ FOLDING FOUR STAMPS

Just by looking, can you tell how many different ways you can fold a strip of four stamps?

You may only fold on the perforations, and the end result must be a stack of four stamps on top of each other.

It does not matter whether the stamps are face up or face down. There are 24 possible permutations of four colors, as shown.

How many can you achieve by folding?

ANSWER: PAGE **124**

▼ FOLDING A SQUARE OF FOUR STAMPS

Just by looking, can you tell how many different ways you can fold a square of four stamps?

You may only fold on the perforations, and the end result must be a stack of four stamps on top of each other.

It does not matter whether the stamps are face up or face down.

There are 24 permutations of four colors, as previously shown.

How many can you achieve by folding?

ANSWER: PAGE 125

▲ FOLDING SIX STAMPS

Six stamps are joined in a 2-by-3 rectangle, which can be folded in many ways along the perforated sides to create a stack of stamps.

The color sequences of four stacks are shown.

Can you tell which stack is impossible to fold?

It does not matter whether a stamp is face up or face down in the final folded stack.

ANSWER: PAGE 125

▼ FOLDING EIGHT STAMPS

Can you fold the block of eight stamps along their perforations so that the stamps are stacked in order from 1 to 8?

ANSWER: PAGE 125

▲ FOLDING NEWS

How many times do you think you will be able to fold a page of a newspaper in half?

Five times? Eight times? More than ten times?

Try it and find out!

ANSWER: PAGE 125

▼ FOLD SQUARES 1

Square pieces of paper are folded in quarters, and then holes are punched through them, as shown in the figures on the left.

When the small squares are unfolded, symmetric patterns are formed.

Can you tell which large square corresponds to each folded-up square?

ANSWER: PAGE **125**

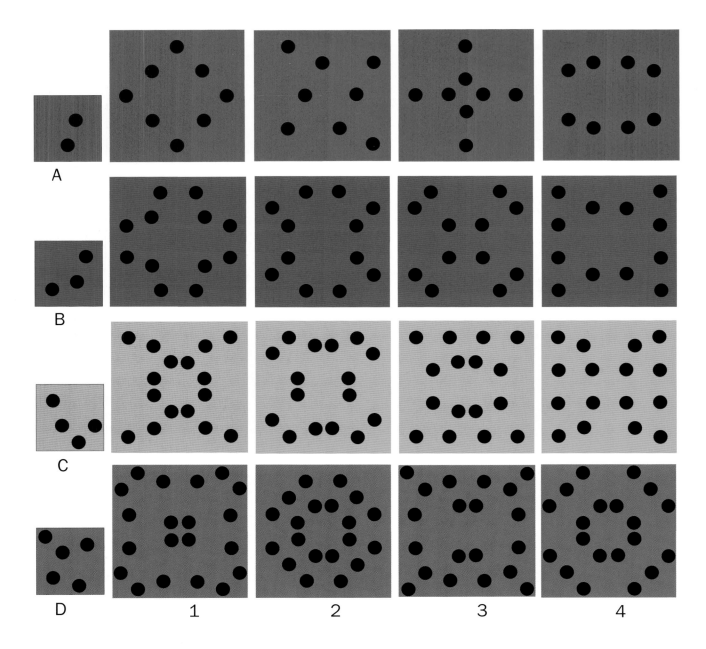

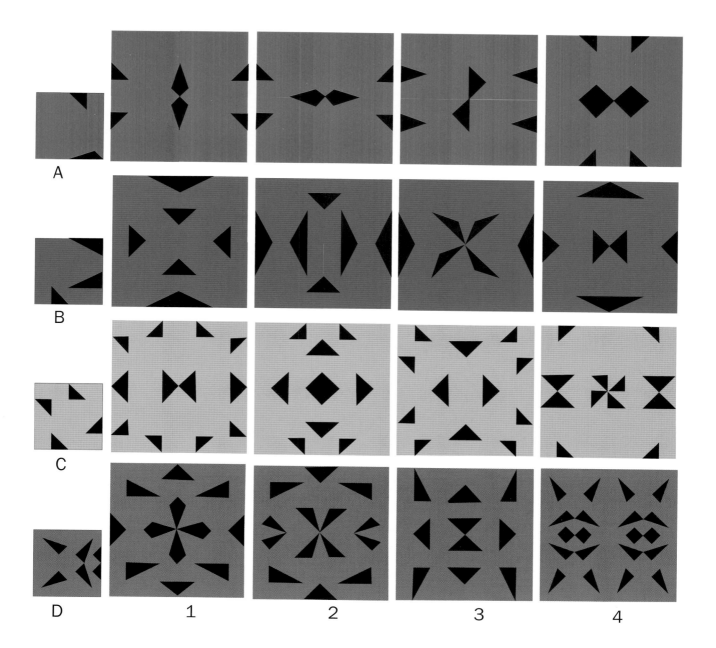

▲ FOLD SQUARES 2

Square pieces of paper are folded in quarters, and then holes are cut in them, as shown in the figures on the left.

Can you tell which large square corresponds to each folded-up square?

ANSWER: PAGE 125

▼ FLEXAGON

We are used to a sheet of paper having only two sides. How can a piece of paper be folded so that it has not two but three sides?

Such a piece of paper is called a flexagon.

Copy, cut out, and glue together the diagram's two sides to prepare the flexagon. Then crease, fold, and tape the folded structure together as shown. (Make sure the tape does not stick to the layer of paper below the panels that you are taping together.) You can then gently fold and unfold the completed flexagon in succession to reveal the three animals without damaging the paper.

Front

fold and glue ➤

Back

PAPER ART

Can you recreate the paper structure below with a single strip of paper? How long does the strip of paper need to be?

ANSWER: PAGE 126

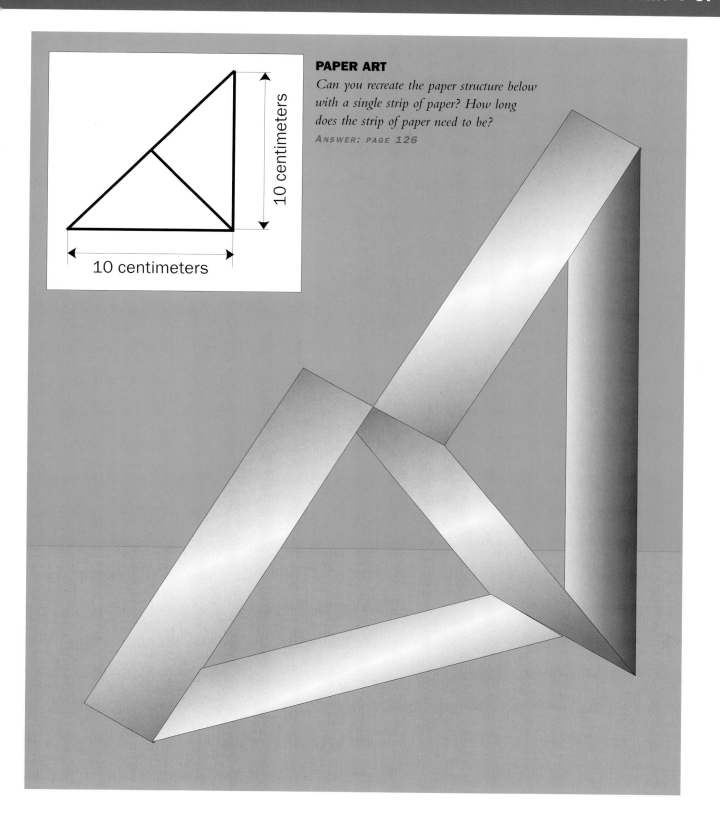

10 centimeters

10 centimeters

▼ TETRAFLEXAGON

Here is a more complicated flexagon—a tetraflexagon, which can be flexed to reveal four different faces. You will discover that finding the fourth figure —the octagon—is quite tricky. But it can be done! (Here is a hint: try to think of other ways the flexagon can be folded and unfolded.)

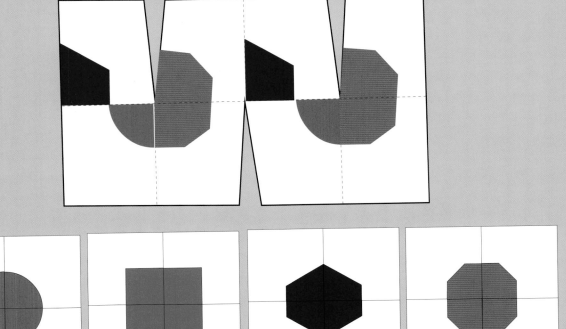

The four faces, with the elusive octagon.

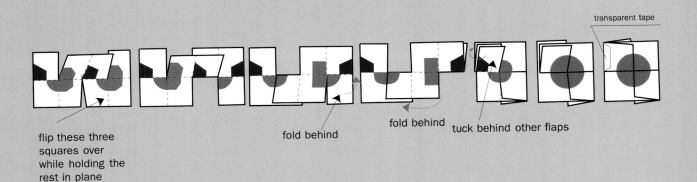

flip these three squares over while holding the rest in plane

fold behind

fold behind

tuck behind other flaps

transparent tape

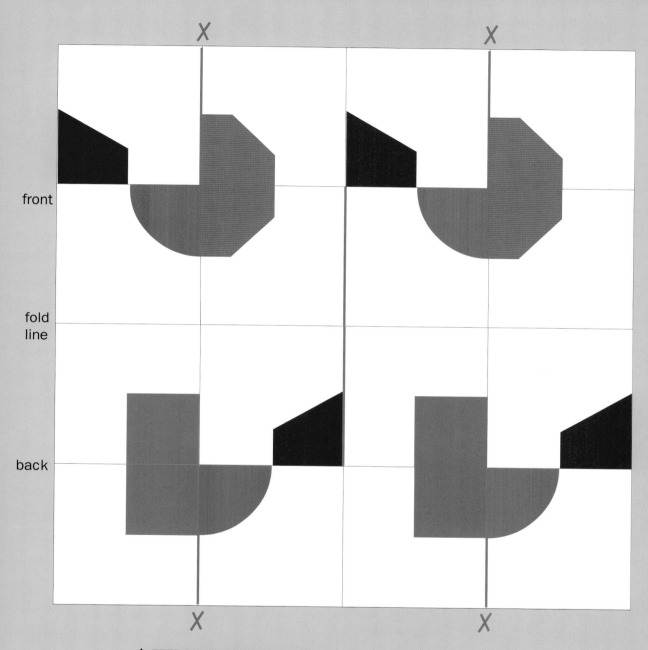

front

fold
line

back

▲ TETRAFLEXAGON DIAGRAM

Copy and cut out the diagram, fold along the fold line so that all the shapes are visible, and glue the two sides together. Then cut three slits as indicated by the red lines.

Crease, fold, and tape as shown on the previous page to form the completed flexagon.

◄ CURIOUS FOLDS

Imagine taking a paper triangle which is yellow on the front and red on the back and folding each corner to its neighbor to make a crease. The three creases which this process creates appear to meet at a point.

Does this always happen whatever the shape of the triangle?

ANSWER: PAGE **126**

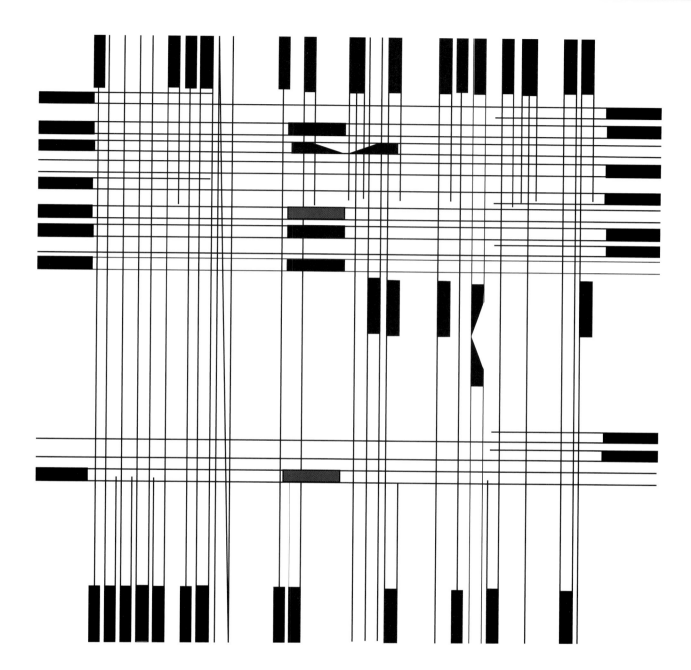

▲ VOLTAIRE'S MESSAGE

Can you read Voltaire's message?

A great French satirist, Voltaire (1694–1778) loved puzzles and created many brain-teasing riddles.

ANSWER: PAGE 128

Some people give up on a problem at a first glance but others, being persistent, feel the satisfaction when a puzzle is finally completed. Which one are you?

◀ IMPOSSIBLE DOMINO TOWER

At first glance this structure seems impossible to build, since it would collapse as soon as the first few bricks were laid. But if you think about it in the right way, you can work out how to do it—and even build it yourself with dominoes.

ANSWER: PAGE **126**

✳ Impossible

If you were to say to a scientist in 1900 that in the year 2000, satellites would transmit pictures to your home, that millions of people would fly through the air every day, and that you could cross the Atlantic at 2000 miles per hour, that man would have visited the moon, that people would carry telephones weighing a few ounces and speak to anyone anywhere in the world without wires, or that most of these miracles depended on devices the size of a postage stamp—if you said all this, the scientist would say "IMPOSSIBLE," and almost certainly pronounce you mad.

Accurately predicting the future is not an easy thing to do, as anyone who tries it quickly learns. History is filled with bold forecasts made by experts that did not quite pan out.

When we say something is impossible, we often don't mean that. What we mean is that we can't see any way to achieve it. Human ingenuity has always overcome apparent impossibilities.

▼ IMPOSSIBLE DOMINO BRIDGE

Here's another structure that at first seems impossible to build. Can you see how to constuct it?

ANSWER: PAGE 126

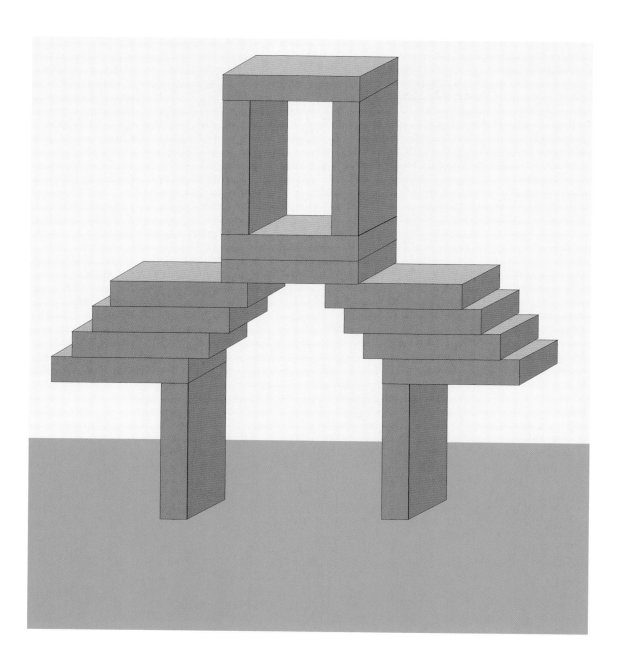

▼ IMPOSSIBLE TASK

*Our flag-bearer was ordered to raise the flag
from the highest point of the tower.
Can you help him find the spot?*

ANSWER: PAGE **128**

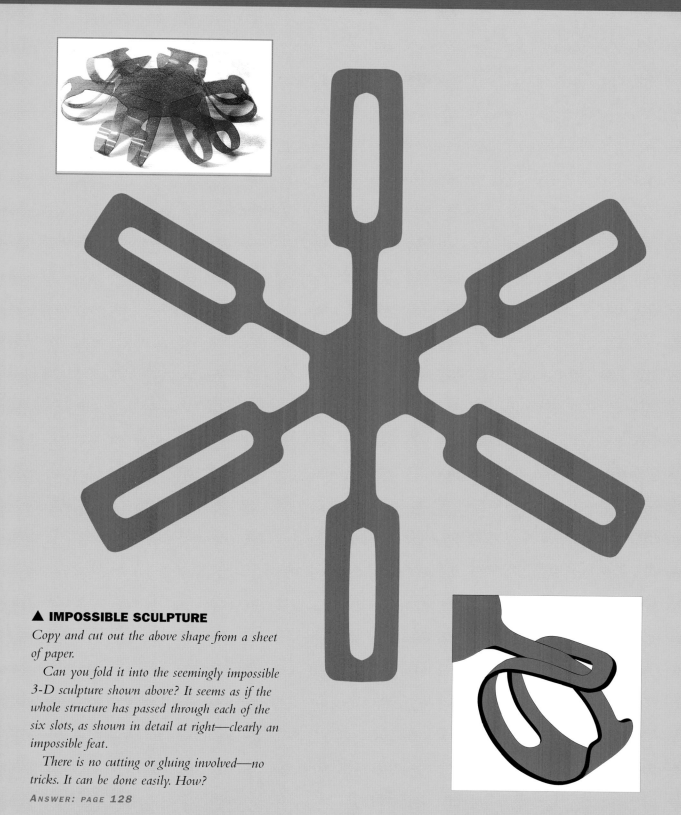

▲ IMPOSSIBLE SCULPTURE

Copy and cut out the above shape from a sheet of paper.

Can you fold it into the seemingly impossible 3-D sculpture shown above? It seems as if the whole structure has passed through each of the six slots, as shown in detail at right—clearly an impossible feat.

There is no cutting or gluing involved—no tricks. It can be done easily. How?

ANSWER: PAGE 128

Don't get dizzy trying to follow the triangles on this page. The spirals may leave you feeling slightly light-headed.

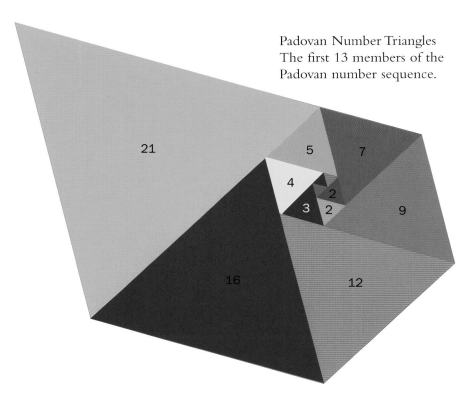

Padovan Number Triangles
The first 13 members of the
Padovan number sequence.

❄ Padovan spiraling triangles

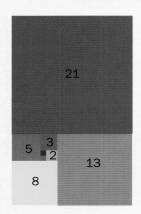

Golden Rectangle
The first 8 Fibonacci numbers.

The famous Fibonacci number sequence (F) in the golden rectangle is formed by spiraling squares of sizes 1, 1, 2, 3, 5, 8, 13, 21, 34, 55, 89, ...

The ratio of consecutive Fibonacci numbers in the sequence gets closer and closer to the golden ratio (which is also known as phi, and which equals approximately 1.61). An analogous progression using spiraling equilateral triangles forms a lesser-known number sequence called the Padovan sequence, after the architect Richard Padovan.

As shown above, the progression of equilateral triangles starts with three unit equilateral triangles: 1, 1, 1, 2, 2, 3, 4, 5, 7, 9, 12, 16, 21, ...

Can you find the general rule for forming the consecutive numbers in the sequence and list the first 22 Padovan numbers? (You can check your answer on the next page.) Comparing the Padovan number sequence with Fibonacci numbers: 1) Are there numbers that appear in both sequences? 2) What is the tendency of the ratios of successive terms as compared to the golden ratio of the Fibonacci sequence?

▼ PADOVAN SPIRALING TRIANGLES

What is the next Padovan number in the sequence?

ANSWER: PAGE 128

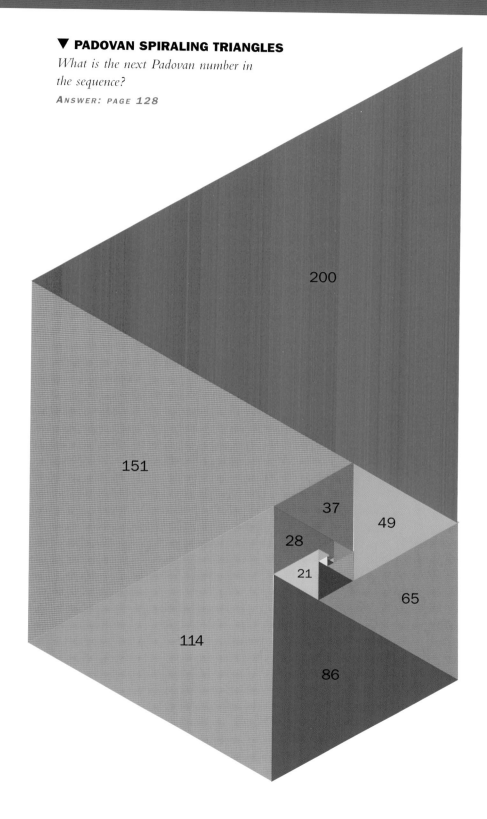

▶ ZENO'S PARADOX (page 6)

The first fault in Zeno's thought process is the assumption that the sum of an infinite number of numbers is always infinite. This is not the case.

The infinite sum of:

$$1 + \tfrac{1}{2} + \tfrac{1}{4} + \tfrac{1}{8} + \tfrac{1}{16} + \tfrac{1}{32} + \tfrac{1}{64} + \ldots = 2$$

This is known as a geometric series.

(A geometric series is a sequence which begins with 1 and whose successive terms are found by multiplying the previous term by a fixed amount (x), which in this case is ½. Infinite geometric series converge to a finite number when x is less than one.

The distance that Achilles travels and the time it takes him to reach the tortoise can both be expressed as an infinite geometric series with x less than one, so the total distance Achilles travels to catch up with the tortoise is not infinite, and neither is the time required.

Suppose Achilles has given the tortoise a 10 meter head start, and Achilles runs at 1 meter per second, ten times faster than the tortoise. It will take Achilles 5 seconds to cover half this distance. Half the remaining distance will take him 2.5 seconds, and so on. He will cover the distance in a finite 10 seconds, according to the converging infinite geometric series.

By that time the tortoise has moved 1 meter. Achilles should pass the tortoise at a point 11.1111... meters from where Achilles started, taking just over 11 seconds to reach that point, and winning the elusive race.

Zeno's paradox gave birth to the idea of convergent infinite series.

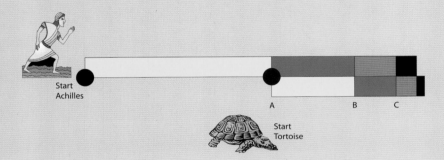

Start Achilles

A   B   C

Start Tortoise

▼ PEGGING HEARTS (page 8)

WHITE BEAR (page 9)

An American psychologist and professor at Harvard University, Daniel Wegner, devised this famous experiment on thought suppression in 1987.

No matter how hard you try not to think of the white bear, you won't be able to avoid the forbidden thought for more than a few minutes at most, when the white bear will again appear in your thoughts.

Wegner explained this phenomenon by an automatic process in the mind. The attempt to suppress a thought, ironically, seems to conjure up a process that then works against the very intention that set it in motion. In any attempts to control our minds, two processes are activated simultaneously: an operating process (to carry out our intention), and an ironic process that works unconsciously, enhancing the sensitivity of the mind to the very thought that is being suppressed.

▶ SQUARE ROOT (page 10)

Draw a line x to form three right-angle triangles as shown.
We then know that the lines have these relationships:

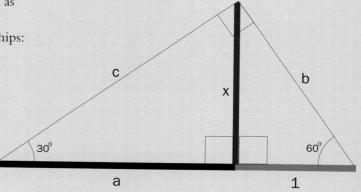

$c^2 = a^2 + x^2$
$b^2 = x^2 + 1$
$(a + 1)^2 = b^2 + c^2$
Substituting the above values for $b^2 + c^2$, we get this equation:
$a^2 + 2a + 1 = x^2 + 1 + a^2 + x^2$
$a^2 + 2a + 1 = a^2 + 2x^2 + 1$
$2a = 2x^2$
$a = x^2$
$\sqrt{a} = x$

ANT PROCESSIONS (page 11)

1) Surprising
2) Surprising
3) Not surprising, because there are two instances of a distance of 2 between a red egg and blue egg.
4) Not surprising, because there are two instances of a distance of 4 between a red and yellow egg.
5) Surprising
6) Not surprising, because there are two instances of a distance of 1 between a red and a blue egg.

▼ **GYMNASTIX (page 12)**

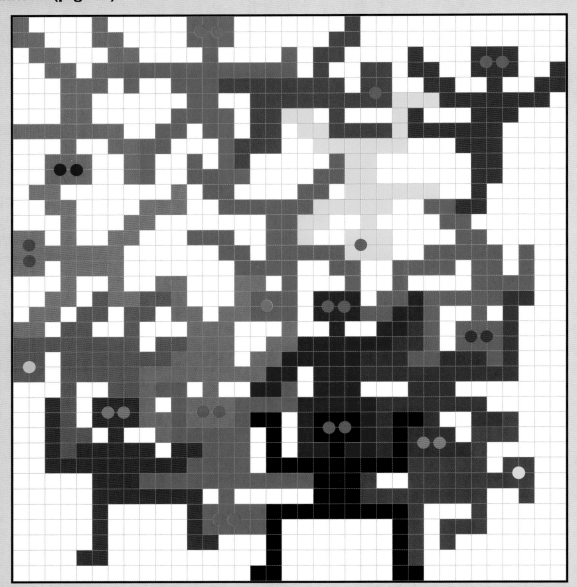

COUNTING DOTS (page 14)

Of course, you could count the dots one by one, but this would take longer than your time limit.

By quickly studying the patterns and grouping of the dots you can do it much more quickly.

Puzzle 1: In each of the 9 smaller squares there are 10 dots—90 dots altogether.

Puzzle 2: In the 10-by-10 square 10 dots are missing—90 dots altogether again.

▶ FIRST EIGHT POLYOMINOES
(page 16)

The five tetrominoes cannot fit into a 4-by-5 rectangle. The T tetromino covers three black squares and one white square. The rest cover two squares of each color. So the five tetrominoes must cover an odd number of squares of each color, but we have ten squares of each color in the board; the problem is therefore impossible.

The first eight polyominoes can be fitted into a 4-by-7 board; one of the many solutions is shown above.

▼ POLYFORM LATIN SQUARE 1 (page 18)

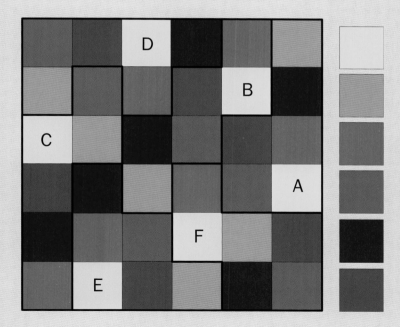

▼ POLYFORM LATIN SQUARE 2 (page 19)

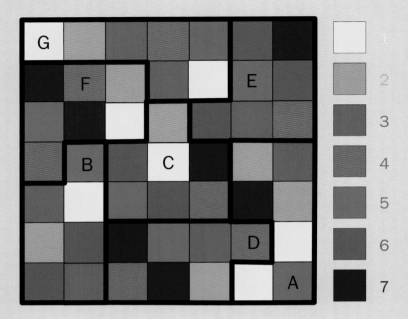

▼ POLYOMINO SYMMETRY (page 20)

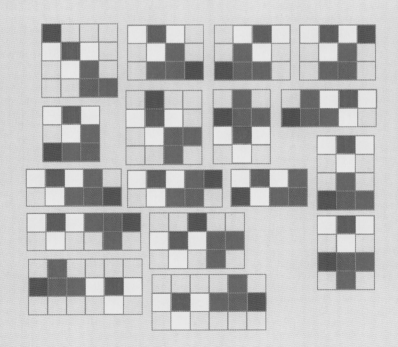

▼ POLYOMINOES TILING RECTANGLES (page 21)

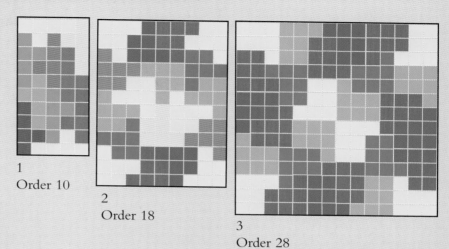

1
Order 10

2
Order 18

3
Order 28

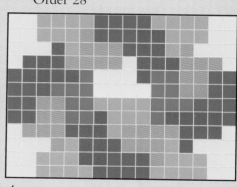

4
Order 24

▼ STEP-BY-STEP (page 22)

There are 32 different configurations.

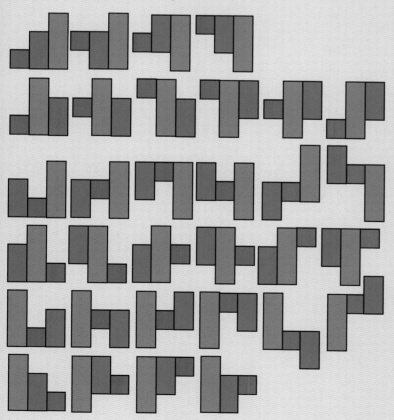

▼ TWELVE PENTOMINOES (page 24)

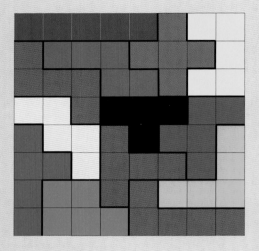

The twelve pentominoes can be placed in a great number of ways on a chessboard, always leaving 4 empty squares. No matter where the four empty squares are chosen, there is always a solution, one shown.

▼ PENTOMINO PUZZLES (page 26)

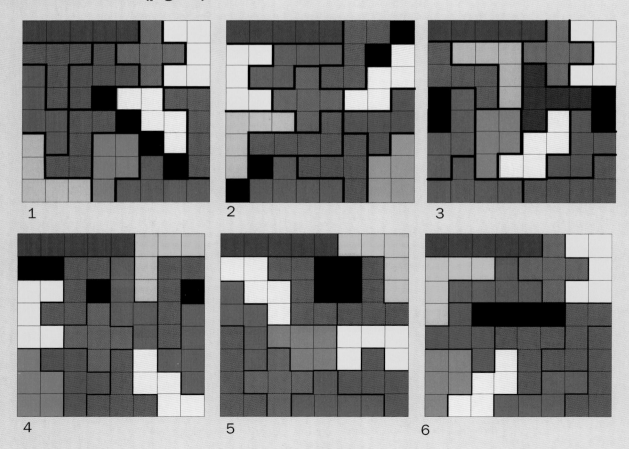

1

2

3

4

5

6

▼ **MINIMAL PENTOMINO PUZZLE (page 27)**

Five pieces.

▼ **PENTOMINO TRISECTIONS (page 28)**

▼ **PENTOMINO TRIPLICATION (page 29)**

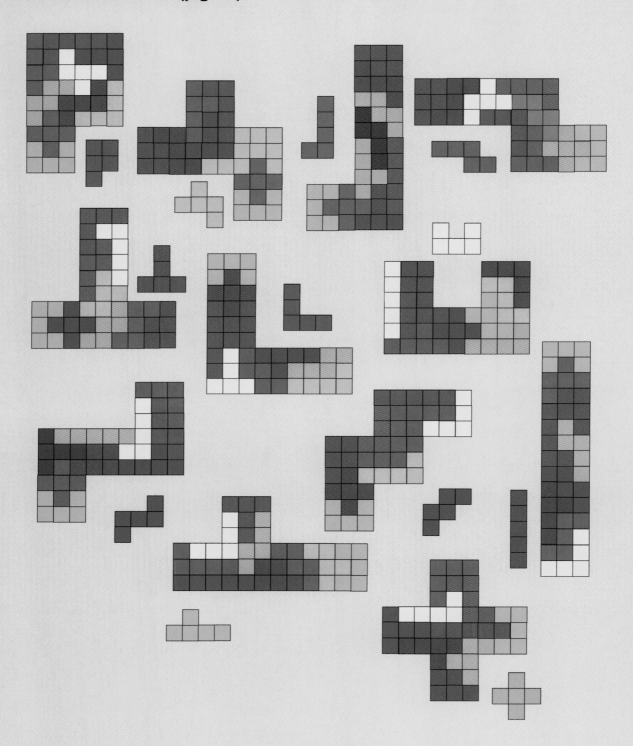

▼ **PENTOMINO FENCE (page 30)**

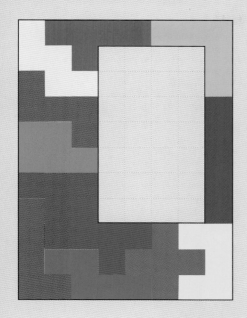

▼ **PENTOMINO FENCE 2 (page 31)**

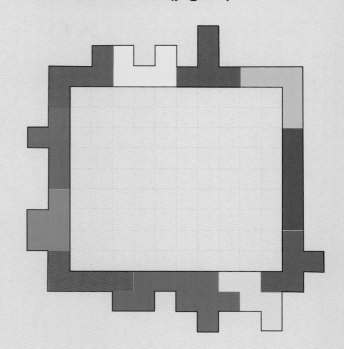

▼ **PENTOMINO FENCE 3 (page 32)**

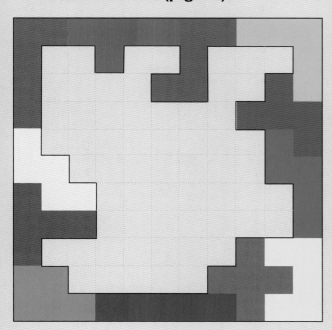

▼ **PENTOMINO FENCE 4 (page 33)**

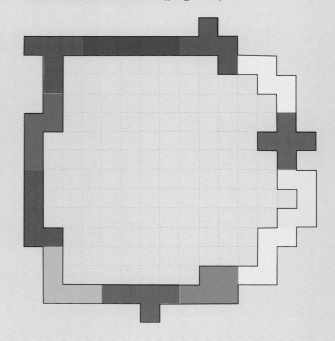

▼ **JAGGED EDGE PENTOMINO GAMES 1–2 (pages 34 and 35)**

▼ **HEXOMINOES (page 36)**

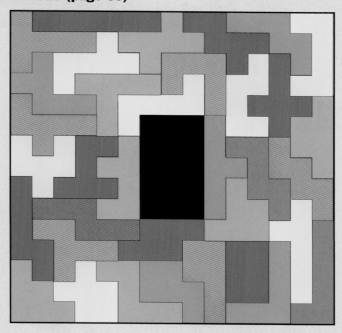

▼ **POLYHEXES (page 38)**

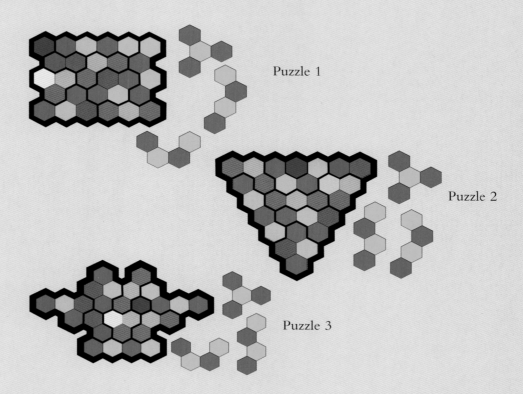

Puzzle 1

Puzzle 2

Puzzle 3

▼ PENTAHEXES (page 40)

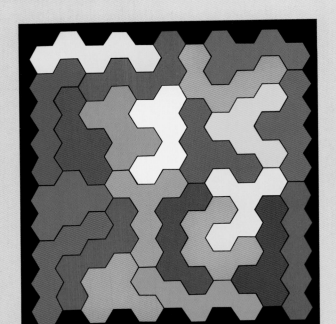

▼ PENTAHEXES DOUBLE PUZZLE (page 44)

▼ PENTAHEXES IN A HEXAGON (page 43)

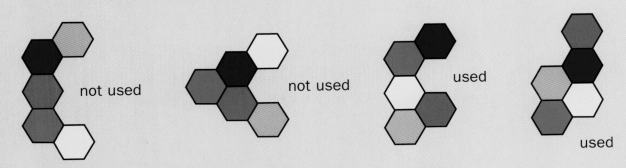

not used   not used   used   used

▼ CHESSBOARD SQUARES (page 45)

There is a total of 204 squares, forming the sequence:

$$8^2 + 7^2 + 6^2 + 5^2 + 4^2 + 3^2 + 2^2 + 1^2 = 204$$

The total number of different squares on a square matrix with n units on a side is the sum of the squares of the first n positive integers.

▼ HEXIAMOND PUZZLES (page 47)

▶ HEXIAMONDS OF O'BEIRNE (page 48)

O'Beirne spent several months trying to find a solution; his first is shown here. How many solutions are there in total? Richard K. Guy classified the solutions. According to his guess, there are about 50,000; there are already more than 4,200 in his collection.

▼ **HEXIAMOND STAR AND HEXAGON (page 50)**

This is the only
known solution for the
hexiamond star.

▼ HEPTIAMONDS (page 51)

▼ TETRABOLO SQUARE (page 52)

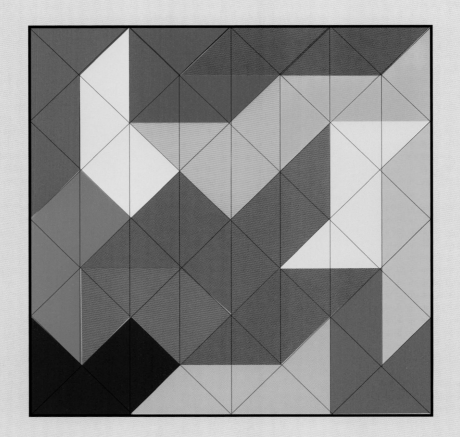

▼ **FISHNET (page 54)**

All 18 of the fishes swimming around the fishnet can be caught as shown.

▼ **MONUMENT (page 55)**

The monument is what is known as a rep-36 polygon.

It can be dissected into 36 identical copies of itself as shown.

▼ PARALLELS (page 56)

All lines are parallel except the line indicated by the arrow. It is tilted to correct the distorting effect caused by the background. This slight modification makes the line indicated by the arrow and the two lines adjacent to it appear to be parallel, when in fact, it is the only line which is not parallel to the rest.

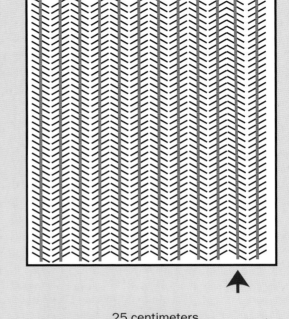

25 centimeters

▶ BOOKWORM (page 57)

The bookworm travels a distance of 25 centimeters as shown, eating through 4 full books, the front cover of volume 1, and the back cover of volume 6

▶ COLORING MAPS (page 58)

While four colors are needed for most maps, maps drawn in a particular way may not need as many. One case is where the maps are drawn using only straight lines.

A little experimenting suggests that two colors are then sufficient. Is this true?

In fact it is true, and the proof is quite easy. Add the lines one by one to the map, As each line is added, interchange the two colors on all regions that lie on one side of the new line. This makes the colors remain different across old boundaries, as well as across the new one.

The same proof can be generalized to apply to maps in which the boundaries are either single curves that run across the whole plane, or closed loops. All these two-color maps have an even number of edges

meeting at any junction. This must be true of any map that can be colored with just two colors, because the regions around a junction or corner must be of alternate colors. Indeed, it can be proved that any map on the plane can be colored using only two colors if and only if all its junctions have an even number of edges meeting there. This is the two-color theorem.

▼ FOUR COLOR HEXAGONS (page 59)

A sample game in which there is no legal move remaining.

One possible solitaire puzzle solution.

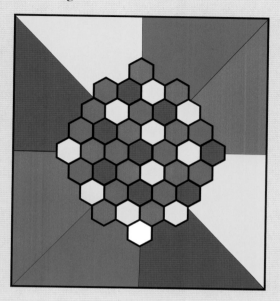

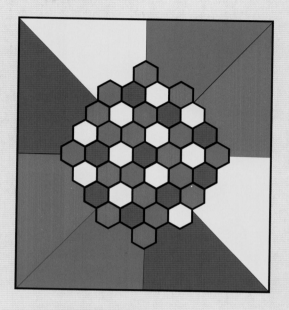

▼ COLORING PATTERN (page 60)

Four colors are needed.

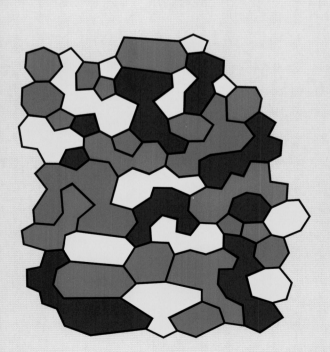

▼ GRAPH COLORING (page 61)

Four colors.

LIFT OFF (page 62)

When lifted in the proper order, the frames spell CREATIVITY.

▼ TRIANGLES IN A SQUARE (page 63)

Twenty identical 1-by-2 triangles forming a square. By repeating this pattern four times in a 2-by-2 pattern, you can make a square from 80 triangles.

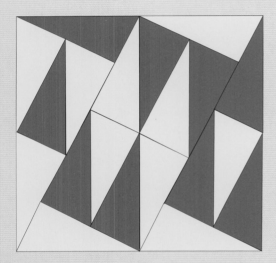

PAPER PENTAGON (page 64)

The surface has one side and one edge. The joined knot achieves a 180° twist of the strip of paper and forms a Möbius strip.

▼ DOUBLE TOWERS (page 65)

17 moves are needed as shown.

▼ CUMAZE (page 68)

▼ **PYRAMAZE (page 69)**

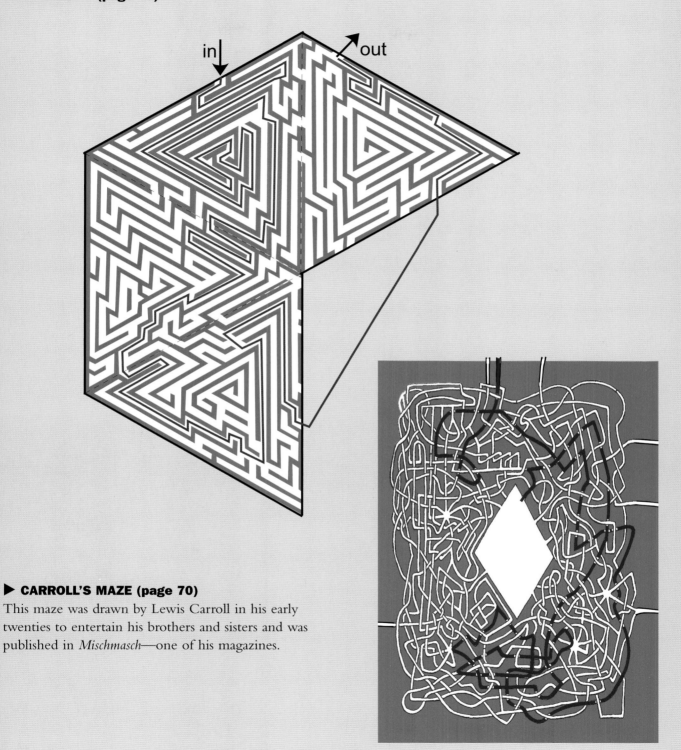

in

out

▶ **CARROLL'S MAZE (page 70)**

This maze was drawn by Lewis Carroll in his early twenties to entertain his brothers and sisters and was published in *Mischmasch*—one of his magazines.

▼ HEX-MAZE (page 71)

▼ SQUARE FOLD (page 73)

Folding a square into four differently sized squares

Fold each corner to the midpoint of the square and you'll get a smaller square. This can be repeated until the paper is too thick to fold.

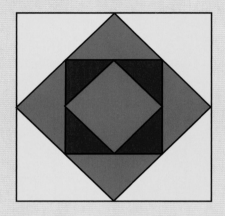

▼ MISSING SQUARES (page 72)

The series represents the sequential folding and unfolding of a square piece of paper, one side of which is yellow and the other red.

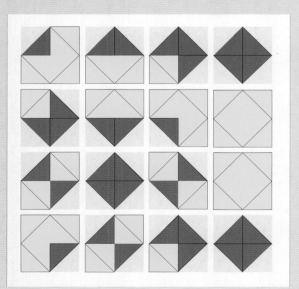

Folding a square into a honeycomb

This works like magic.

Roll the square into a cylinder and then, using two fingers, press along the length of the cylinder alternately changing the angles by 90 degrees each time. When you unfold the paper you will have an orderly tessellation of hexagons.

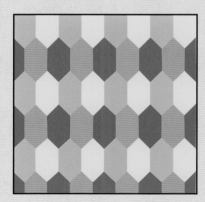

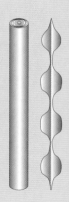

▼ **SQUARE FOLD continued (page 73)**

Folding a square into a regular octagon

1) Fold each corner of a square piece of paper to the midpoint to form a smaller square as shown:

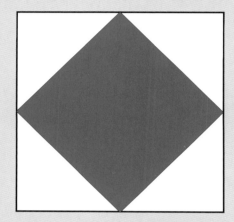

2) Then take each corner and fold so the edge of the paper touches the edge of the smaller square, bisecting the angle as shown. Do this eight times.

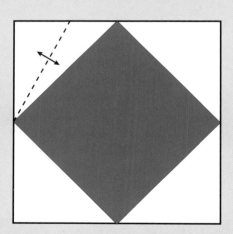

3) The points at which the eight folds you've just made intersect form the corners of an octagon. But is it a regular octagon?

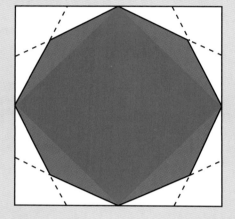

4) Four of the angles consist of a corner of the internal square (90°) plus two bisected 45° angles (22.5° each): 90° + 22.5° + 22.5° = 135°

The other four angles are each one angle of a triangle, and the other two angles of that triangle each equal 22.5°. The angles of a triangle add up to 180°, so: 180° − 22.5° − 22.5° = 135°

All eight angles are therefore equal and the octagon is regular.

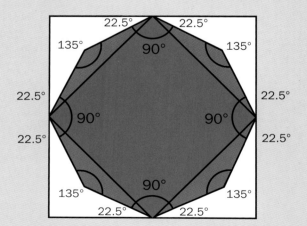

▼ SOKOBAN (page 74)

A 23 move solution.

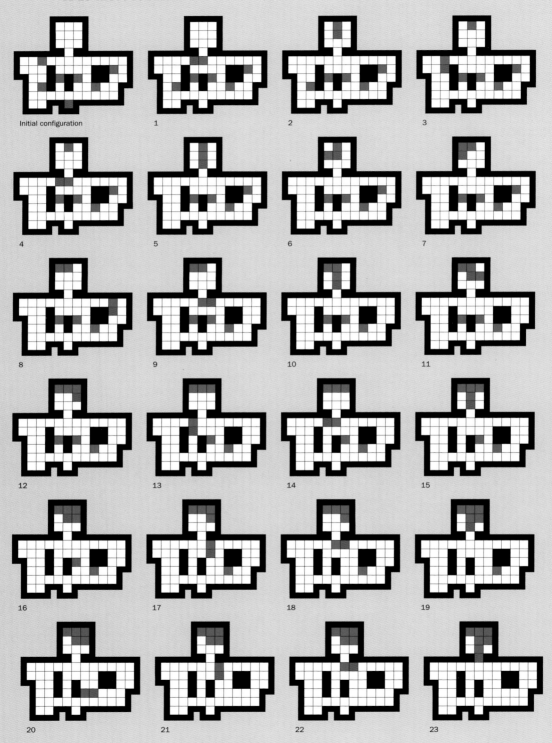

▼ HAMILTON'S PATH (page 76)
Other solutions are possible.

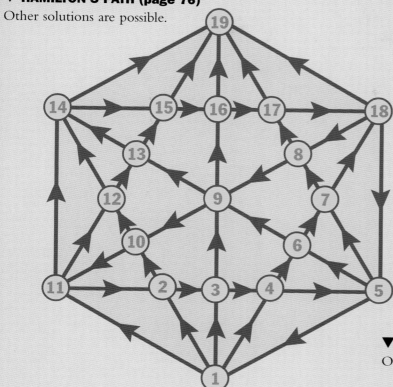

▼ HAMILTON'S LOOP (page 77)
Other solutions are possible.

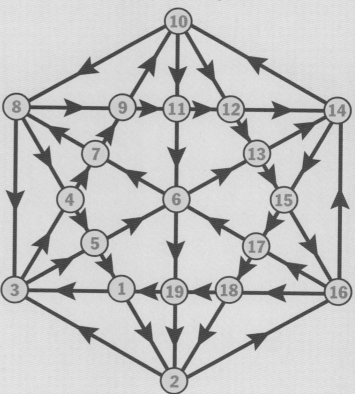

▼ FOLDING THREE STAMPS (page 78)

You can achieve the complete set of 6 permutations by folding.

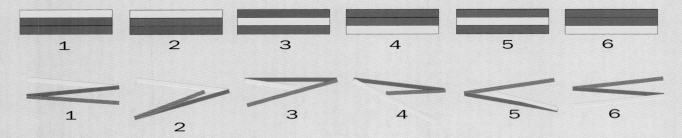

▼ FOLDING FOUR STAMPS (page 79)

16 of the 24 permutations are possible.

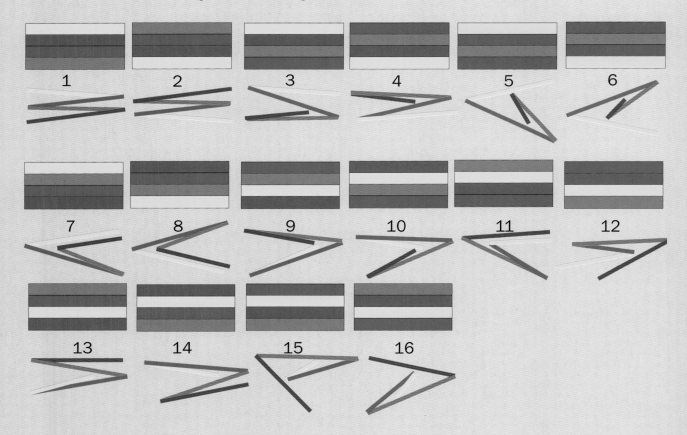

▼ **FOLDING A SQUARE OF FOUR STAMPS (page 80)**

Eight of the 24 permutations are possible to fold.

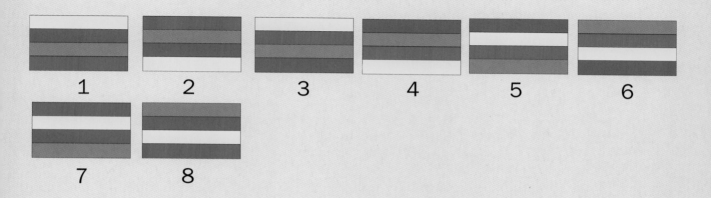

FOLDING SIX STAMPS (page 81)

Fold 3 is impossible.

It is not possible to fold the strip to make diagonally adjacent colors adjacent in the final stack.

FOLDING EIGHT STAMPS (page 82)

Fold the right half of the sheet below the left half so that 5 is above 2, 6 is above 3, 4 is above 1, and 7 is above 8.

Now fold the bottom half up so that 4 meets 5, and 7 meets 6.

Then tuck 4 and 5 between 3 and 6, and fold 1 and 2 on top of the stack.

FOLDING NEWS (page 83)

It is practically impossible to fold a page of a newspaper in half more than eight times, no matter how large or thin the sheet is.

This is because each fold doubles the thickness of the paper—a process which makes the paper get very thick very quickly.

After eight folds, the thickness of the paper is 256 times as thick as it was at the start. This thickness prevents further folding, unless you are one of those muscular giants who is able to perform such feats.

FOLDING SQUARES 1 (page 84)

A–4

B–1

C–1

D–3

FOLDING SQUARES 2 (page 85)

A–1

B–2

C–3

D–4

▶ **PAPER ART (page 87)**

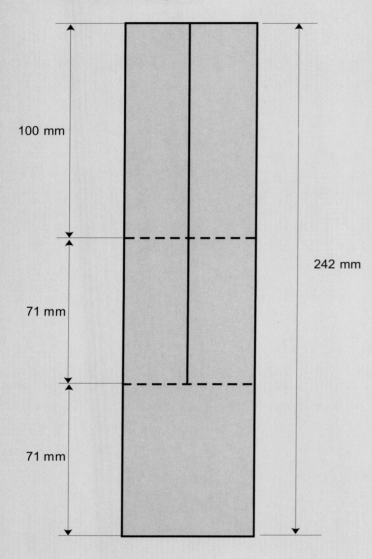

100 mm

71 mm

71 mm

242 mm

▼ **CURIOUS FOLDS (page 90)**

Yes, but why?

What you actually did by folding the paper was to create three perpendicular bisectors on each side of the triangle. These always meet at a point called the circumcenter of the triangle. This is the point from which you can draw a circle circumscribing the triangle, passing through the three vertices.

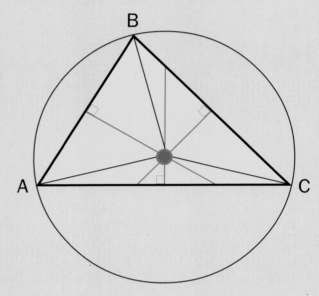

VOLTAIRE'S MESSAGE (page 91)

Hold the page at eye level to read the message:

"ILLUSION IS THE FIRST OF ALL PLEASURES"

IMPOSSIBLE DOMINO TOWER (page 92)

The secret is to start with three dominoes set vertically as a temporary base. The two outer dominoes can be removed at the end when the structure is built and well-balanced.

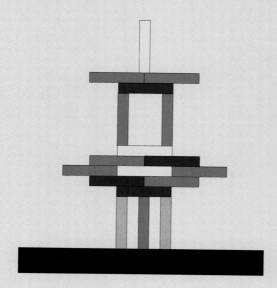

IMPOSSIBLE DOMINO BRIDGE (page 93)

Some scaffolding may help! Place two of the blocks in temporary supportive positions, as shown in the diagram. When the bridge is almost complete, move the blocks to their final position on top.

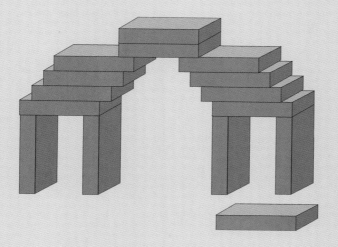

▶ IMPOSSIBLE SCULPTURE (page 94)

Repeat the sequence at right six times to create the impossible sculpture.

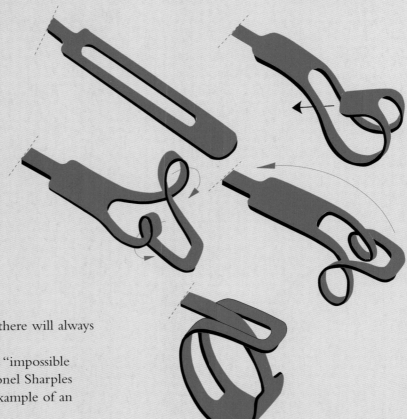

IMPOSSIBLE TASK (page 95)

No matter what point you choose, there will always be a higher spot.

The castle is based on the famous "impossible staircase" introduced in 1958 by Lionel Sharples Penrose and Roger Penrose as an example of an impossible object.

PADOVAN SPIRALING TRIANGLES (page 97)

The first 22 Padovan numbers:

1, 1, 1, 2, 2, 3, 4, 5, 7, 9, 12, 16, 21, 28, 37, 49, 65, 86, 114, 151, 200, 265, …

The general rule of forming the Padovan sequence: Each number in the Padovan sequence is the sum of the second and third preceding numbers.

The first 21 Fibonacci numbers: 1, 1, 2, 3, 5, 8, 13, 21, 34, 55, 89, 144, 233, 377, 610, 987, 1597, 2584, 4171, 6755, 10925, …

The only numbers belonging to both sequences are 3, 5, and 21.

The ratios of successive terms of the Padovan sequence approach the plastic constant (P), whose approximate value is 1.324718. It bears the same relationship to the Padovan sequence as the golden ratio does to the Fibonacci sequence.

Is it possible that future discoveries may reveal the appearance of Padovan numbers in nature. This occurred with the Fibonacci series, which was originally just a man-made recreational mathematics puzzle.